David Hepworth has been writing, broadcasting and speaking ~~~ ~~~ music and media since the seventies. He was involved in the launch and editing of magazines such as *Smash Hits*, *Q*, *Mojo* and *The Word*, among many others.

He was one of the presenters of the BBC rock music programme *The Old Grey Whistle Test* and one of the anchors of the corporation's coverage of Live Aid in 1985. He has won the Editor of the Year and Writer of the Year awards from the Professional Publishers Association and the Mark Boxer award from the British Society of Magazine Editors.

He lives in London, dividing his time between writing for a variety of newspapers and magazines, speaking at events, broadcasting work, podcasting at www.wordpodcast.co.uk and blogging at www.whatsheonaboutnow. blogspot.co.uk.

He says Chuck Berry's 'You Never Can Tell' is the best record ever made. 'This is not an opinion,' he says. 'It's a matter of fact.'

For more information on David Hepworth and his books, see his website at www.davidhepworth.com

Praise for *Uncommon People: The Rise and Fall of the Rock Stars*

'[A] colourful, richly marinated survey of the phenomenon of the rock star . . . After almost an adult lifetime of witnessing the music industry at close quarters, Hepworth is, in many ways, a dream author' *Guardian*

'A celebratory but multifaceted look at this strangest of occupations' **** *Mojo*

'*Uncommon People* attempts to preserve this vanishing breed in a kind of rock star bestiary . . . A composite biography of an almost folkloric figure, one made of bits of Bob Marley and Madonna, Prince and Ian Dury' *Sunday Times*

D1428469

Also by David Hepworth

1971 – Never a Dull Moment
Uncommon People – The Rise and Fall of the Rock Stars
A Fabulous Creation

NOTHING IS REAL

THE BEATLES WERE UNDERRATED AND OTHER SWEEPING STATEMENTS ABOUT POP

David Hepworth

BLACK SWAN

TRANSWORLD PUBLISHERS

61–63 Uxbridge Road, London W5 5SA
www.penguin.co.uk

Transworld is part of the Penguin Random House group of companies
whose addresses can be found at global.penguinrandomhouse.com

First published in Great Britain in 2018 by Bantam Press
an imprint of Transworld Publishers
Black Swan edition published 2019

A CIP catalogue record for this book
is available from the British Library.

ISBN
9781784164072

Typeset in 10.81/15.18pt Minion by Jouve (UK), Milton Keynes.
Printed and bound in Great Britain by Clays Ltd, Elcograf S.p.A.

Penguin Random House is committed to a sustainable future
for our business, our readers and our planet. This book is made
from Forest Stewardship Council® certified paper.

1 3 5 7 9 10 8 6 4 2

For Poppy and Alice

CONTENTS

Contents

Contents

ACKNOWLEDGEMENTS

Thanks to Mark Ellen, who edited some of these pieces in their original form in *The Word*; and to Trevor Dann, who produced the series of *Nothing Is Real* essays, and Matthew Dodd, who commissioned them for BBC Radio 3.

Thanks also to my agent Charlie Viney of the Viney Shaw Agency, and Bill Scott-Kerr, Darcy Nicholson, Richard Shailer and Sally Wray of Transworld.

website   www.davidhepworth.com
blog   whatsheonaboutnow.blogspot.co.uk
Twitter   @davidhepworth

INTRODUCTION

We called him Uncle Stan. He wasn't really our uncle but that's what we called him. He would come and visit us at Christmas. Uncle Stan came from the other side of the Pennines, wore a cardigan with suede facings, worked as a salesman and was, by the standards of our house anyway, smooth. He smoked filter-tipped cigarettes, had his own smart hi-fi at home and believed that Frank Sinatra had said all there was to be said in popular music.

Uncle Stan singled me out because he liked to tease me about my gauche enthusiasm for music. At Christmas 1963 he visited as usual and said to me, as usual, 'What record have you got for Christmas this year?' I proudly showed him my treasured copy of *With The Beatles*, which had come out a few weeks earlier. This was the Christmas of Beatlemania.

To the adults of the day Beatlemania seemed no more likely to be remembered in the future than the Christmas of the Mutant

Ninja Turtles would seem to me when I had my own children to tease. Uncle Stan couldn't resist what seemed like an open goal. 'Let me tell you something,' he said, reaching into the pocket of his Dean Martin cardigan for his Ronson lighter. 'When I come next year and I ask you the same question you'll have forgotten all about the Beatles.'

Of course Uncle Stan came the following year. And of course when I met him I was brandishing my new copy of *Beatles For Sale*. He returned in 1965 and I was able to greet him with *Rubber Soul*. At Christmas 1966 I brightly proffered my copy of *Revolver*.

By 1967 the poor man had given in and ruefully conceded that if only he had chosen to illustrate his point about the ephemeral nature of pop music with the example of the Dave Clark Five or Gerry and the Pacemakers he might have hit the bullseye. Instead through sheer ill luck he had landed on the act who were to the era of pop what Frank Sinatra had been to the era of the big bands – the exception that proves the rule.

At the time even the idea of a career writing about pop music was a distant fantasy I didn't dare entertain. When it came to pass, in the mid-seventies when I was fulfilling my slightly less distant dream, that of working in a record shop, it was mainly exciting because it gave me access to the odd free album, which was the way I interpreted all questions of worldly wealth at the time. When that led eventually to a full-time job title containing the word 'editor' I still didn't think it could last, any more than Ringo thought that his moment in the spotlight would last.

That was in 1979. I've spent the almost forty years since then writing about, editing magazines about, broadcasting about and pontificating about pop music. Some of those pieces are reprinted here. In some cases I've rewritten or added to them. Some were composed off the top of my head, as the best blog entries invariably are, while others were arrived at after prolonged chin-stroking, as befits essays to be broadcast by the most august wing of the BBC.

Quite a few of them touch upon the group that caused Uncle Stan such embarrassment back in the mid-sixties. Since then the Beatles have been the fixed point of my musical universe. I was one of the generation shaped by them. It wasn't just their music. It was the way they did everything. I can remember the thrill of first seeing them on TV. I can remember the pride I felt when they stormed the citadels of the adult world – the London Palladium, Buckingham Palace, even the United States of America. I can remember the inevitability of their break-up. I can remember long periods in the seventies when nobody thought about them much. Then I remember the second Beatlemania that followed the death of John Lennon and their subsequent taking up by generations who weren't born in that six-year window when they did the things they did.

With groups like the Beatles – not that there are any groups like the Beatles – there's a danger of the weight of their story distracting us from the piercing joy of their music. You could say something similar of someone like Frank Sinatra – not that there was anyone like Frank Sinatra. In the case of both, the difference is all still in the records for those with ears to hear. That's where this book begins. Half a century on from those Christmases with Uncle Stan the Beatles burn as brightly as ever.

London, 2018

1
THE LONG SHADOW
OF THE FABS

THE BEATLES WERE UNDERRATED

In the course of our forty-five-year love affair with the Beatles, something important was lost. Their craft became obscured by their artistry, their artistry disappeared into their significance and their significance was eventually folded inside their legend. The result is that they are underrated for the work they did and overrated, if anything, for what it all meant.

Louis Menand's Iron Law of Stardom holds that no show-business career can be sustained for longer than three years. After that time creativity is exhausted and public affection begins to flag. Menand defends his theory against Beatles exceptionalists by pointing out that they actually had a six-year career divided into two: three years as cheery moptops immediately followed by three years as psychedelic adventurers.

It's this second period that tends to impress us most these days.

That's the one focused on by critics in the rock magazines or people of Noel Gallagher's generation. It's not a complete surprise. There's a perceptible stylistic link between the White Album and, say, Paul Weller. This is immediately evident to the contemporary eye and ear. A few years ago an Oasis-loving friend of mine decided to buy a Beatles record to see what the fuss was about. He bought *Let It Be* and was disappointed. He admitted later that he'd actually bought that one because its cover showed them looking most like his idea of a contemporary rock band. Like my friend, a lot of people are only comfortable with the Beatles when they appear to be serious, edgy, hip, and thus of today.

While that second three-year career is not without its delights, the first period was actually when the Beatles' collective genius was operating at full tilt. To fully appreciate it from the vantage point of today we have to shrug off our infatuation with fashionable gloom and shed the illusion that true artists are all complex and impenetrable. We must accept the fact that the greatest pop group of them all didn't consider it beneath them to make their records for fourteen-year-old girls. When they made their classic records the false opposition between rock and pop hadn't yet been invented. The wall between the two has been the refuge of scoundrels and snobs ever since. To appreciate why we still underrate the Beatles you have to shrug off that prejudice and travel back to 1963, when they were far from a done deal.

For a start, there were things the Beatles did first. They took the previously discrete skills of singing, songwriting, arrangement, A&R, backing instruments and production and conflated all into the one skill – creating great records. Nobody had done that before.

The records they made were often better than the songs

deserved. The Beatles weren't great songwriters, at least not like Cole Porter was a great songwriter. Many of their lyrics are banal in the extreme. They were only interested in writing the songs insofar as they knew songs were a vital ingredient of great records.

They combined the qualities of a good vocal group with the skills of a capable instrumental group. The fusing of two previously separate competences created a new musical shorthand and explains why they sometimes seemed to be putting more into the record than there was room for.

When their time came they were ready. As Malcolm Gladwell pointed out in his book *Outliers*, they had ten thousand hours of live experience behind them before they saw the inside of a recording studio.

They were the epitome of a group. 'Groupness' is not about having the people best qualified to discharge a certain role in a group. It resides in how well these people make up that group. The jibe attributed to Lennon about Ringo not even being the best drummer in the Beatles was off the point. Even if Ringo was not the best drummer in the Beatles, he was certainly the best drummer for the Beatles.

Then there was Lennon and McCartney: two lost boys who somehow transformed their differences into the greatest creative dividend of all. Unlike most partnerships where creative tension is allegedly at work, they managed to avoid discouraging each other. While clearly capable of loathing from time to time, it was the contributions each made to the other's ideas that struck the sparks. At their best they were like magnets in balance, holding the iron filings of the Beatles' music in perfect suspension.

Then there's the stylistic stuff. They were clever without

suffering from education – often a handicap for a pop musician. They were from the English provinces in an age when that seemed to be a barrier you could never surmount without a Pygmalion transformation. In his 1964 book *Love Me Do!*, the American journalist Michael Braun even suggested that to the media and the London-based establishment they were actually a new kind of people.

None of this accounts for the fact that well over forty years later I'm writing this. There's something else – above, beyond and beneath all this ballyhoo. At the heart of the Beatles saga is the key ingredient of popular music success, the element that people spill bitter sweat to achieve, rarely credit when it's present or fully note when it's absent, and certainly never give enough weight to in critical histories. This element accounts for the waxing and waning of every career in popular music. It is, as far as pop musicians are concerned, the spark of life at the end of God's outstretched finger, without which all their greatest efforts are naught. It is the simple but devilishly elusive quality we can only apologize for calling catchiness.

Traditionally, catchiness is a measure of how memorable a tune is, particularly the first time on the ear. When it comes to making records rather than songs, this is an inadequate definition. Lennon and McCartney could noodle their way to a good tune. But they didn't stop there. Some compulsion or restlessness or fear made them come up with another tune, hook or melodic idea complementary to the original one, something they could build into their song. Their records are strewn with details that anyone else would have been happy to base a complete record on. The coda of 'Hello Goodbye' is one such. The prequel to 'Here, There

And Everywhere' points to another ballad altogether. Their early albums are full of wonderful songs they never put out as singles because they didn't think they were quite number one material. It's been said before but it bears regular repetition: 'Penny Lane/ Strawberry Fields Forever', which is on many people's lists of the best singles ever, was left off *Sgt. Pepper*, which is on many people's lists of the best albums ever, because they had more good tunes than they knew what to do with.

The richness of their golden period has never been equalled. I can remember hearing the first radio play of 'We Can Work It Out/ Day Tripper' in the winter of 1965. Many acts can devise a tune that's catchy. What really hooks the listener is the promise of further layers of catchiness to come. I knew there was enough on the glistening surface of 'We Can Work It Out' to be going on with but I was also aware of something in that deliberately ungainly middle section that would tug away at me for a longer time. Because they had such flair for arrangement, such ears for the telling junction, their records were full of neat, thrilling transitions that became hooks in themselves. The listener would ricochet from one hook to another like a metal ball in one of Bally's machines.

I had the same feeling in the summer of 1967 when I first heard Kenny Everett play tracks from *Sgt. Pepper* on the radio. There was more than enough in 'Lucy In The Sky With Diamonds' to enchant on first hearing but there was also a promise that the enchantment wasn't going to wear itself out easily. Nothing in pop music is more powerful than a thrill containing the promise of further thrills. Between 'All My Loving' and 'Penny Lane' the Beatles made at least twenty records that managed that rare trick. In doing so they redefined catchiness.

This serial approach to catchiness provided its own unique rush of joy. All their mid-sixties chart-toppers gathered intensity as they went along. Even when the song was supposed to be the heartfelt plea of a broken man, as in 'Help!', they delivered it with bracing glee. Even when they started leafing through the *Tibetan Book of the Dead* in 1966 they were still taking 'Tomorrow Never Knows' at a rare clip. They never idled away their efforts on long instrumental intros. There was no foreplay. Listen to 'All My Loving', 'Penny Lane', 'Eight Days A Week' or 'No Reply'. 'Help!' begins like a leap from a high cliff which immediately goes into a steep climb. It was as if they knew the secret of a good speech – start in the middle and finish soon afterwards. They began every number as if the shepherd's crook of time was about to hoick them off stage and deposit them back at the dole office in Liverpool.

While writing this I got my record deck out and played their original 45s and mono LPs. The whole house was energized by the sounds, teenagers and all. This is music aimed at simply making people happy. Sadly for rock critics, it's not complicated. In the early cover versions the headlong dash to delirium was signalled by the yowl of joy announcing every guitar break. In their own songs it was achieved by more sophisticated means, such as the climbing middle eight in 'No Reply'. All their middle eights, such as Lennon's 'when I was a boy' in 'She Said She Said' or Paul's 'me I'm just the lucky kind' in 'Things We Said Today', offer renewed injections of the quality they managed to exude naturally or synthesize so well you couldn't tell the difference: optimism. Cheer was what pop music was traditionally supposed to offer, just as the movies today are meant to provide a thrill ride. I recall a radio jingle that used to describe 'the happy sounds of Radio 1'. They wouldn't be allowed to say that today even from within a thicket of inverted commas. Nowadays happiness makes people uneasy.

The Beatles were war babies, born into times a good deal harder than ours, even right now. The music their parents danced to was intended to make them forget their daily troubles, whether that meant the food they didn't have or the bombers overhead. The music the Beatles played as young men was about providing ecstasy in three-minute hits. But it was still accepted that daily life was dull and full of care. As standards of living have inexorably risen and peace has continued in the near half-century since they broke through, as the undemanding excitement of the sixties and seventies has given way to the anxious torpor of our connected society, it's probably inevitable that we've become more blasé. Because we never grow out of pop music we have to somehow invest it with adult qualities in order to justify it to our adult selves. Nobody uses the word 'happy' in connection with pop nowadays unless it's to sneer.

I recently visited Studio Two at Abbey Road. It was never a promising birthplace for the greatest run of hit records in history. The parquet floor reminds you of a school hall from the fifties. The four Beatles began recording here in September 1962 and stopped in the summer of 1969. The first few Beatles records aren't very good and the last few are solo records. But somewhere in between, in a period that starts in July 1963 (when they recorded 'She Loves You' and most of their first great long-player *With The Beatles*) and ends when the four of them record 'Getting Better' in March 1967, the last of the Abbey Road records that really sounds like a group, they came to this room to do the work on which their reputation rests. In 1968, sensing what they had lost when they stopped playing together, they made 'Get Back', a record which suggested this would be impossible. There was no way back into the secret garden of Studio Two. There was no regaining that unique balance between sophistication and simplicity. But it's still there for us if we're prepared to take it in the spirit it was intended. Because if you're too cool for the records they made in that room you really are too cool.

P.S. The above was a piece I wrote for *The Word* in 2008. It was an attempt to rescue the Beatles from beneath the dead weight of all that cultural significance and point out that what made them exceptionally good was the catchiness of their records, particularly the early ones. I subsequently received one reader's letter which was so derisive that I almost felt like turning up on his doorstep.

This chap's argument seemed to be that the Beatles' greatness was so Olympian it couldn't possibly be reduced to mundane matters of craft. How could the word 'catchiness' possibly do justice to their achievements?

I'll tell you how. I subsequently saw an excellent documentary called *The Wrecking Crew*, about the Los Angeles session musicians of the sixties and seventies. It features the reminiscences of people like Hal Blaine, Carol Kaye, Tommy Tedesco, Earl Palmer, Plas Johnson and Glen Campbell, the people who played the actual music on everything from 'River Deep Mountain High' through 'Somethin' Stupid' to Herb Alpert's 'The Lonely Bull'. It's like going under the bonnet of a whole era of peerless pop music, from the Byrds' 'Mr Tambourine Man' to the theme from *Hawaii Five-0*, while the engineers explain what makes it tick.

To hear musicians Carol Kaye and Al Casey talk about how they arrived at the backing sound of 'These Boots Are Made For Walkin'' is to realize how much of a hit record's emotional stickiness arises from the uniqueness of a particular performance. This in turn owes a huge amount to the idiosyncratic ear of a certain musician. Nancy Sinatra has performed that song thousands of times since that recording date but she hasn't found anyone who can play the distinctive bass line like the combination of Chuck Berghofer on string bass and Carol Kaye on electric did on that day. 'It's very difficult to capture,' she says. Capture's the word.

The Wrecking Crew proves how wrong my Beatles correspondent was. And I think most rock fans are probably every bit as wrong in exactly the same way. They think greatness in pop is all about soul and inspiration and having your heart in the right place. It's not. It's about the tiny details that, in the words of a musician interviewed in the documentary, 'make the tune pop'. If it doesn't pop, all the elements – song, singer, musicians and that unspecified box of skills which we in our ignorance summarize under the word 'production' – just lie there on the slab.

When these musicians used the word 'pop' it was as a verb, not a noun. That's my learning for the week. Nobody knew better than the Beatles how to make something pop.

IT'S ALL ABOUT THE DRUMMER

When Ringo Starr arrived with the rest of the Beatles at the EMI studios in Abbey Road for their first proper recording session in September 1962 he found to his surprise and dismay that another drummer was already in there, setting up his kit. This drummer was Andy White, a trusted session man. White had been called in by George Martin, a producer experienced enough to know that very often when a new group got into the studio for the first time it was the drummer who let them down.

Although the tune they were recording that day, 'Love Me Do', didn't call for any particular fireworks in the rhythm department he couldn't be sure that Ringo, who'd only been recruited recently, could handle the task. He'd heard the previous drummer, Pete Best, who was a bit of a plodder, and couldn't be certain that the new man was any better. The presence of the other drummer led to a tense opening session and got the relationship between George Martin and Ringo Starr off to a shaky start, from which they never quite recovered. Even decades later Ringo would revisit how slighted he felt when he saw that other drum kit.

Drummers always take it personally, which says a lot about why drummers are so special. In the words of a musician friend of mine, drummers know where the beat is. The people at the front may have written a wonderful song, arranged it imaginatively and embroidered it with their instrumental and vocal brilliance, but it's the rude mechanical at the back who decides where the beat is. And it won't be a decision he'll reach as the culmination of a rational process. It won't be anything you can persuade him about. It will be a decision his body and brain will reach for him on the basis of his physiological make-up and he'll be no more capable of changing it than he is of altering the way he walks, kicks a football or the shape his body adopts when sleeping. Other musicians perform the music. Drummers *are* the music.

This can make the other musicians very resentful and probably accounts for the fact that drummers are the butt of cruel jokes such as 'What do you call somebody who hangs around with musicians? A drummer', and so on unto infinity. It's not surprising that in the seventies drummers fought back against this culture of disrespect by surrounding themselves with more and more equipment and developing a repertoire of tricks and gimmicks which gained the respect of other musicians for the simple reason that they looked difficult. This also resulted in the development of that most uncalled for musical digression, the drum solo. The drum solo is the auditory equivalent of being unable to find the exit from a multistorey car park. It doesn't matter how good the drummer is, the only person not praying for the solo to come to an end is the person who's playing it.

Great drumming is, like the internal combustion engine, something we only truly value when it's not working. And when it's not working the only thing you can do is get another drummer. Which is what the Beatles did when they tired of Pete Best and got Brian Epstein to fire him so that they could bring in Ringo. Epstein said it was only when Ringo joined that the picture seemed complete, which was a shrewd observation to make. If you go back and listen to those pre- and post-Ringo recordings you can hear how even within the limitations of a rudimentary rock and roll style Ringo sends the blood coursing through the band's veins in a way his predecessor would never have done if he'd remained on that drum chair for the next ten years.

Just as Ringo was the last to join he was also the first to leave, walking out during the White Album sessions in the summer of 1968 because he felt that he wasn't valued. One of the reasons he wasn't valued is because he never did anything to draw attention to himself. Ringo's musical style was of a piece with his personal style. It was all self-effacement.

It's only in the last ten years, once we'd grown up enough to realize how empty and flashy all that jazz-rock and progressive soloing was that beguiled us at the end of the sixties, that we've come to realize what a blessing Ringo's drumming was. He revolutionized rock drumming by eschewing the chopsticks grip which people like the Shadows' Tony Meehan had inherited from big band players like Gene Krupa in favour of holding both sticks like hammers, the better to make an impression on the snare and on the customers at the back of a crowded dance hall. But when he got to the studio Ringo proved to have a lot more subtlety than anyone suspected.

Again this had its basis in his physical make-up. He was born left-handed but his grandmother was superstitious and wouldn't allow him to use his left hand. Therefore he learned to play on a right-handed kit but always had to begin his fills with the left hand. This is the reason why no other drummer can imitate what he does on 'Ticket To Ride' from *Help!* or 'Come Together' from *Abbey Road*. In the time it took him to get from one area of the drum kit to another he would create pauses which were every bit as much a part of his style as the times when his sticks were coming into contact with the skins.

In its sixty-year history rock has gone from simplicity to pointless elaboration and back to simplicity again. We now realize that judging a guitar solo by how fast it's played is like judging a novel by how quickly it was typed, and we now know that the best drummers are the ones who do something that you can't replace with a machine.

Smart opinion invariably gets pop music wrong, praising it for qualities that matter in other art forms and passing over the things that matter most in pop. That's why smart opinion sees the Beatles as two great songwriters plus help, rather than the four-headed euphoria machine that they were. That's why smart opinion listens to Marvin Gaye's 'I Heard It Through The Grapevine' and hears a soulful evocation of betrayal and loss rather than a slow groove that makes everyone dance like a night-time prowler that the police believe could help them with their enquiries.

Critical opinion has been listening to rock the wrong way round and it's about time this changed. It's about time we faced the reality that whereas not all pop music is rock and roll and not all rock and roll is pop, it is all essentially rhythm music. The only term that I think can satisfactorily encompass both these plus disco, reggae, electronica, funk, rhythm and blues and all the rest of the sub-divisions that often bewilder us is 'beat music', which is the term that we used to use in the mid-sixties before everybody demanded a term that flattered their enthusiasm and made it seem more important. It is all beat music. You can tell because it calls for a physical response, whether that means full-blown dance fever or just tapping your fingers on the steering wheel. All the things that jazz and classical fans don't like about beat music, the repetition and dumb simplicity, those are the very things that are best about it. If you don't like the beat, you don't like the music and you should go and find something else to like.

So now that we know that the most important men in beat music – and they were mainly men – were the men who provided that beat, we should give them their due. Men like Earl Palmer, who invented rock and roll drumming in the fifties when he imported the bass drum sound of the New Orleans parade band into the hits of Fats Domino and Little Richard. When in later life some wet-behind-the-ears indie band asked him if he could play along with them, he said with justification, 'I invented this shit.' Hal Blaine, who provided the most dramatic three beats in popular music, the ones that introduce the Ronettes' 'Be My Baby'. Richard Allen and Uriel Jones, who played that drum track on Marvin Gaye's 'I Heard It Through The Grapevine', the one you can hear in your head right now if you close your eyes. Charlie Watts of the Rolling Stones, who understood that you play slightly behind the band so that you sound as if you're reining them in rather than whipping them on. And who else? Well, not many others. John Bonham of Led Zeppelin, he whose sound has been likened to a wardrobe full of bricks being tipped down a concrete staircase and has been sampled for use on a million hip hop records. Levon Helm of the Band, who was a double threat because he could sing as well. Clyde Stubblefield of James Brown's band, the man who inspired the tune 'Funky Drummer'. Carlton Barrett, the man behind the snare drum crack on those Bob Marley records. Each one had a fingerprint as unique as, well, a fingerprint. We shall not hear their like again.

One of the reasons we shall not hear their like again is that the producers of today get round the problem that George Martin was anticipating back in 1962 by replacing the drummer with a drum machine. Most of the records you hear on today's chart weren't so much recorded as assembled. They start with a rhythm track and then they layer effects on top of that track. They are not relying on a mere human being to achieve that particular rhythmic state of grace that led to 'Come Together' or Roxy Music's 'Love Is The Drug'. The percussion on today's hits is programmed, usually very skilfully, to achieve the sort of efficiency the producer is seeking. You can see why they do it. Nothing speeds up or slows down, as it might have done when the drumming was the responsibility of a weak and feeble human being. And people who've grown up to expect the regularity of a digital world they expect no less of music. Old actual drum sounds are simply part of the palette, flown in from time to time to provide a taste of alleged authenticity like a microwaved meal served up on a plank. But there's no point getting nostalgic. Music has moved on. It's now made by machines, which is not a criticism. Pop music has always been driven by technology, and today's no different.

The age of the drummer has passed, and the least we can do is recognize that it was the age of the drummer. It started in the mid-fifties and lasted until the early nineties. Most records during that time were made by small groups of musicians playing together in studios, groups who were heavily reliant on the man at the drum kit to come up with something that injected life into their otherwise clumsy fumblings. In return, these drummers became the butt of jokes such as the one about the drummer who asked the band leader whether he wanted him to play too fast or too slow, jokes which all mask the other musicians' anxiety that all their efforts might be as naught without this element which looks so easy to do and yet clearly isn't, which almost anyone could do adequately and hardly anyone can do well, which cannot be fixed in post-production, and which in the end counts for more than the efforts of all the other musicians put together.

The story is told that one day word reached Charlie Watts in his hotel room that Mick Jagger had been asking, 'Where's my drummer?' downstairs. Charlie set aside the sketch pad in which he was recording the details of his hotel room. He got dressed in his best three-piece suit with stiff collar and tie, cashmere socks, hand-made shoes and the rest. Once he was properly attired he went down to the bar where he found Jagger, grabbed him by the lapels, forced him against a wall and, stabbing him in the chest for emphasis, said, 'Don't you ever call me your drummer. You're my singer.' And having made his point, and the point this column has been trying to make, he tossed him aside, left the bar, went back to his room, took off his suit, put on his lounging uniform and took up his pad to resume doing what he does every day while on tour, which is to sketch the details of every hotel room he occupies. Yes, that's right. I said that drummers were underrated. I never said they weren't strange.

P.S. I'm no musician but I've always been fascinated by how bands operate. Although the drummer is the one who is the butt of the jokes from the rest of the band, the drummer is also the one they can never manage to replace. The likelihood is the thing that made them successful in the first place owed an enormous amount to the way the drummer played and the way he made the rest of them play.

That's why there was never any chance of Led Zeppelin keeping going after John Bonham died. He was the one who dictated how the rest of them played. That's why the Who without Keith Moon are missing more than just a drummer. That's why the Ramones were never the same after Tommy Ramone stopped playing the drums. That's why nobody but Levon Helm could ever have been the drummer of the Band. These people weren't just good players. They decided how the band should walk. The other musicians may have complained about it but in the end they had to get in step.

The 2012 documentary about Status Quo provides the perfect demonstration of this truth. The line-up that made their classic rock shuffles, which they admit were based on the Doors' 'Roadhouse Blues', was Francis Rossi and Rick Parfitt on guitars, Alan Lancaster on bass and John Coghlan on drums. Lancaster left in 1985 and Coghlan in 1981. 'They wanted to replace me with a drum machine,' he recalls, probably inaccurately. It doesn't matter whether it's true. All that matters is he thinks it's true.

Quo soldiered on without Coghlan (and no group embodied that verb more perfectly) but, as Lancaster points out, the albums were just no good any more. They brought in other drummers, who were probably more technically adept, and they even had hits, but old-time fans knew that something was missing. Lancaster started a new life in Australia and got some startling new teeth. Coghlan took his hangdog expression into a variety of bands. Until recently.

The last five minutes of *Hello Quo!* are its best. Here the four original members are reunited on a Shepperton sound stage. They embrace as awkwardly as any other bunch of Brits in their sixties who have been told to do it for the cameras. You get the impression Rossi is the difficult one and Parfitt is the diplomat. Then they take up their instruments and play 'In My Chair'. This is one of those slow, loping shuffles which made their name in the early seventies.

The effect is magical. Suddenly Status Quo is back in the room. The swing has returned. It's not just another bunch of musicians doing their best to replicate a sound that the original four stumbled upon in 1970. It's the sound itself. It's a sound that all rock bands think they can make, which is where all rock bands are wrong. When you hear the real thing you know how wrong they are. Here it is again, forty-two years later, as if by magic. Actually, it is by magic. How else do you describe the way these four individuals just happen to lock together while thousands of other four-man groups, no more or less deserving, simply don't? Rock is not an adjective. Like pop, it's a verb.

MANAGERS ARE THE REAL VICTIMS

O f all the clichés that come streaming into people's heads when they think about the music business the one that dies hardest is the image of the archetypal manager. People only have to mouth those three syllables and a cartoon cloud pops up above their heads into which is sketched a picture of an older, balder man with a cigar jammed in the corner of his mouth, cackling quietly to himself as he counts out the £50 notes he has swindled from the efforts of his saintly, otherworldly charges.

In films about rock bands managers are almost invariably depicted as thieves, philistines and charlatans. I'm not saying this is all balls, but it's mostly balls. When I think of the word 'manager' I don't think of the bald thief counting out the fifties.

I think instead of all the many real-life managers I have known, most of whom were just as unsuccessful as most of the musicians they managed. I think of the many journalists I've known whose love of a band drew them into a Paul McGuinness–U2 relationship with the object of their affections. Unlike the aforementioned they didn't end up with a mansion on a hill. In many cases they ended up with extra mortgages on their modest homes, mortgages that had been racked up in order to pay for costs incurred on the band's nth profitless club tour.

I know people like to think of the manager as the one who sucks the blood from young necks. In my experience it's quite often the opposite. Young bands understandably search out a manager who's got the things they haven't got – a job, a bank account, credit cards, transportation, clean linen, a family, a full fridge, access to a solicitor, somewhere to doss – and then proceed to help themselves to as much of this as they can.

Three things drive young men to form bands: the desire to spend as much time as possible playing music; the belief that this might put them in the way of lots of sex; and the urgent need to avoid having to do any of the things that the world traditionally requires of adults. A manager is invaluable in this regard in that he's the person to whom they can devolve all the many things they find too tiresome to do themselves. They take advantage of his ability to do things they can't be bothered to do, like making appointments, reading contracts and being where they're supposed to be at the appropriate time, and then reserve the right to snigger behind his back because he's done the things that needed doing. When Brian Epstein started managing the Beatles he had the usual motivations – he wanted to be part of their success and he was in love with at least one of them. He hung around long enough to hear the love of his life sing the line 'Baby, you're a rich fag Jew' with apparent relish. There's your payback.

Epstein lasted longer than his modern counterpart would. Very often the manager who gets a band started is cast aside very early in their career. In the old days of record contracts it was common for managers to be ditched as soon as they had negotiated the first deal because the record company preferred dealing with an old hand. The manager might be best out of it. If anything goes wrong in the band's career, the manager's the first to blame. If anything goes right, that's down to their genius. More often than not, managers are the real victims of the great rock and roll swindle. They don't often get a second chance to atone for early mistakes. The act can get over a number of false starts; the managers are usually too busy paying off the debts to start over.

I was reminded of this when I bumped into an old hand the other day. He used to manage an act I knew. 'Oh, him,' he said, talking about the charismatic frontman. 'Horrible, horrible man – though not without talent. Amplifiers used to go missing, bits of kit. He's still involved in the same business – what nowadays I think we call "stealing".'

A HARD DAY'S NIGHT
FIFTY YEARS ON

Fifty years ago this week I went to see *A Hard Day's Night* at the Pioneer cinema in Dewsbury. The Pioneer was situated on the top floor of the Co-op and was reachable via a very slow lift behind a metal grille. In those days nobody took any notice of a film's starting time. You might turn up halfway through, watch until the end and then stay to watch it from the beginning. I watched *A Hard Day's Night* three times that day. It was enthralling.

It was enthralling because it showed the Beatles on a screen yay high and brought them up this close. Nothing had done that before. TV still had end-of-the-pier production values so we had never seen them via a medium that matched their splendour. Cinema tickets, unlike records, were affordable. That's why the release of *A Hard Day's Night* was a moment of greater impact than the release of the two albums they put out before its soundtrack. Everybody shared it.

Last night I went to a screening of a new digital version of the film at the BFI. The director Dick Lester was interviewed by Beatles authority Mark Lewisohn. Lester pointed out that it was only made because the music division of United Artists saw it as a way to get a best-selling soundtrack album; it was shot in black and white because they didn't think Beatlemania would last long enough to justify the investment in colour; and the brass at the company thought it was good but assumed the dialogue would be dubbed to make it more intelligible to an American audience. They were told this would not be possible, not least because there simply wasn't time. There's nothing in media and entertainment that can't be ruined by more money and more time. There's no better illustration of that principle than *A Hard Day's Night*.

I find its comedy a bit leaden nowadays. There's one joke in the film and it goes like this: Don't grown-ups say some strange things? Whether it's Richard Vernon's 'I fought the war for you' routine or Wilfrid Brambell's Irish republican pub talk, Victor Spinetti's overwrought luvviespeak or Kenneth Haigh's assumption of the voice of 'yoof', the message is this is a middle-aged world in which the young people are only occasionally allowed to feature. The fans in the crowd scenes are all wearing Famous Five clothes – pleated skirts, cardigans, winter coats and clumpy shoes – as if they've been decked out for a school concert. They're children.

However, I now realize that the music is even better than I thought it was at the time. I also see that Lester's great achievement was in finding a way to deliver their performances to the screen and happening upon a template which still haunts anyone who tries to point a camera at a pop group. 'If I Fell' and 'I'm Happy Just To Dance With You' are the original and most powerful pop videos because they depict the Beatles ostensibly rehearsing for their TV appearance. That means they're playing but also working and just enjoying being together. They exchange looks that say, right now we're the luckiest people in the world. It's that feeling that they're playing for their own delight that laid down the way all bands would seek to behave even to this day. Lester talked about how they had an indivisible solidarity that saw them through. They're the Beatles and you're not. 'I hope I managed to communicate how I felt about them,' says Lester. He did.

There was such outrageous vitality in their music at the time that it didn't need overselling. The vibrancy of the 1964 sound would never be surpassed. It's amazing that they could do it. In the midst of the madness of Beatlemania they wrote and recorded thirteen absolutely brilliant songs for the film. That's seven to go on the soundtrack and another six you can put on side two. Nobody had ever done that before. Nobody's done it since.

The uncanny perfection of 'If I Fell' and 'I Should Have Known Better' endures after everything else has gone. It filled that luxurious cinema last night as surely as it warmed the Pioneer in Dewsbury fifty years ago this week. We sat there rapt. When the cowbell came in on the middle eight of the title song I felt the screen was about to burst with joy.

RUBBER SOUL FIFTY
YEARS ON

Back in 1965 albums, or 'LPs' as we called them then, were not the key unit of popular music. LPs were usually for Christmas and were so far beyond the disposable income of the average teenager that you could only buy one when you had accumulated enough ten-bob notes and record tokens from aunts. Pop was all about the seven-inch 45 and although we had no idea of this at the time, 1965 was the annus mirabilis of the pop single.

A list of the UK number one singles from that year proves that beyond all doubt: the Righteous Brothers' 'You've Lost That Lovin' Feelin'', the Kinks' 'Tired Of Waiting For You', the Byrds' 'Mr Tambourine Man', the Walker Brothers' 'Make It Easy On Yourself' and Sonny & Cher's 'I Got You Babe' alongside three from the Rolling Stones, including '(I Can't Get No) Satisfaction', and two from the Beatles, both from the soundtrack of *Help!*, their second film, which had been released in the summer. No less influential in that year were gems like Bob Dylan's 'Like A Rolling Stone', the Who's 'My Generation', the Beach Boys' 'Help Me, Rhonda' and the Four Tops' 'I Can't Help Myself'. Because the Beatles had always looked primarily to black musicians for inspiration they would also have been aware that 1965 had seen Wilson Pickett's 'In The Midnight Hour', James Brown's 'Papa's Got A Brand New Bag' and Otis Redding's 'Respect'.

The tour the Beatles undertook after the release of *Help!* climaxed with the show at Shea Stadium in New York in August when they appeared in front of fifty-five thousand teenagers, none of whom could either see or hear them. It was an unprecedented experience which made it clear that the technology of live performance couldn't keep up with the demand to see them. On the same visit they took a few days off in a rented house in Hollywood. They met their idol Elvis Presley, with whom they found it difficult to strike up a rapport, and their fans the Byrds, with whom John and George bonded over acid and Indian music. Following the tour they took six weeks off, the longest break they'd had since the madness began, reconvening at EMI in Abbey Road in mid-October to make an album and a single for the Christmas market.

Rubber Soul, which they finished a month later, was released on 3 December. It was the first Beatles record in which it was possible to detect them being influenced by the torrent of adventurous music they had inspired in others, from the story songs of Bob Dylan to the droning rock of the Kinks, from the bass-heavy Southern funk of Otis Redding to the Chelsea swagger of the Rolling Stones. During 1965 the bar had been raised on a weekly basis. The Beatles closed the year by raising it all over again and proving self-consciously what they had already proved by accident with records like *A Hard Day's Night* – that it was possible to make long-players that were every bit as taut and compelling as singles.

In many ways the album was recorded in the same way they had always recorded. George Martin was the producer, Norman 'Hurricane' Smith the engineer, and they could still only use four tracks. This meant that if they wanted to introduce new instruments, such as the sitar on 'Norwegian Wood' or the harpsichord sound on 'In My Life', they had to 'bounce down' what they had already recorded to a single track, in order to free up tracks for over-dubbing.

They began to ignore the old working practices whereby sessions had always been three hours long. The last session for the record went through the night – a good indication of the way things would be done in the future. However, they hadn't yet gone their separate ways as composers: the middle eight of 'Norwegian Wood', which was John's song, came from Paul; similarly the middle eight of 'Michelle', which was predominantly Paul's, was provided by John. The age gap which separated John and Paul from George was evident in the way McCartney would redo George's guitar parts if he didn't think he was playing them well enough.

They were still a proper group. Although the experience of being a Beatle was bound to make anyone cynical they were still evidently the same brilliant little band who took as much pride in harmonizing the 'la-la-la's on 'You Won't See Me' and got as much fun out of the lascivious inhalation after the title of 'Girl' or the cod-French of 'Michelle' as they did out of the apparently weightier inclusions such as 'In My Life' and 'The Word'. Being easily bored themselves, the Beatles went to enormous pains to make their own records tedium-free.

They finished mixing the record at dawn on 15 November. As usual they were only bothered about the mono mix, leaving the stereo to George Martin and the engineers. The record was in the shops less than three weeks later, which explains why it had an immediacy almost worthy of the social media age. I remember seeing the cover in a shop window from the top of a bus. Its green cast, the covetable suede jackets they wore, along with the artfully distorted logo (provided by Charles Front, father of the actress Rebecca) indicated that once more they had managed to place themselves slightly ahead of the pack. They were still the Fabs, albeit they had turned a little fuzzy at the edges.

My copy arrived on Christmas Day and I played it for forty-eight hours straight. It was the unique genius of the Beatles that their pop appeal was not easily worn out. There was always another layer of texture beneath. Once you had exhausted its knowingness its heart was there to nourish you. At the same time as they were making *Rubber Soul* they had also produced a single; not just any old single but a double A-side; and not just any old double A-side but 'Day Tripper' backed with 'We Can Work It Out'. Hence they finished the year of the single with the number one single as well. There was nothing they couldn't do.

Obviously everybody thinks the music made when they were fifteen was the best music of all. It's not my fault that I happen to be right.

2
POP'S GREATEST DECADE?

Obviously I remember the sixties. Not the distant land of lost content beloved of contemporary TV directors where pretty girls in Courrèges boots are perennially whizzing through the streets of new towns in Mini Mokes accompanied by handsome young men in antique military uniforms intent on enjoying consequence-free sex, but the real sixties. At the time it didn't feel any different from the fifties. The TV was still in black and white, the food was terrible and nobody had any money.

I don't remember anyone marking the tenth anniversaries of major sixties events but I can remember how strange it felt when *Sgt. Pepper* was honoured in this way twenty years ago. This seemed like a new frontier for pop nostalgia. Even at that stage I don't think anyone guessed that fifty years after the event the sixties would still be, in modern parlance, a thing.

Pop history seems to slow down the closer it comes to the present. The Beatles got from 'Love Me Do' to 'A Day In The Life' in four years, which is the interval between Olympic Games. Nothing seems to move that quickly nowadays. It seems to take that long to mix a record. But that might be just my perspective. When I reflect that I'm typing this fifty years after the release of *The Graduate*, that seems only the day before yesterday. It's only when I subtract a further fifty years from the date of *The Graduate* and realize that would take me back to late 1917, when the First World War still had another year to run, that I appreciate how long ago it really is.

The decade beginning in 2010 marked the semi-centennial of the sixties, which provided lots of opportunities to reflect on just how unique a time that was. Of course what the TV image makers and nostalgia-mongers get wrong is that in our heads we are always slightly younger than our physical age and mentally we're always still living in the previous decade.

This particularly applied to the people who made their names in the sixties and carried those newly famous names forward into another fifty years of fame: they were all still children of the forties and teenagers of the fifties, shaped by the decades immediately after the war. Bob Dylan would in time become exasperated by people asking him about being the voice of the sixties because the decade that he knew best was the fifties. Similarly, as far as John Lennon and Paul McCartney were concerned nothing would ever equal the impact of or improve upon Elvis Presley and Little Richard.

In interviews their incident-packed, many-garlanded, post-fame careers often seemed to be to them a kind of dream, the sort of thing they came to rely on others to chronicle on their behalf. It was only when they reached back into the fifties, when they were mere civilians before they were hit in the small of the back by fame, that life seemed real.

THE SUMMER
THE SIXTIES BEGAN

Fifty years ago this week, in the last week of August 1962, the last summer of the old world was drawing to a close. Nobody knew it at the time. Nobody knew that the following year, 1963, was going to see the assassination of John F. Kennedy, the Great Train Robbery, Beatlemania, Martin Luther King's 'I Have A Dream' speech and Bob Dylan singing 'Blowin' In The Wind'.

During that summer of 1962, in Liverpool, Chelsea, Kingston (Jamaica), Los Angeles and New York, an assorted handful of young people were plotting their individual careers, although they wouldn't have dared call them that. They didn't dream that anyone would care the following year, let alone fifty years later.

On 16 August 1962 the Beatles sacked their drummer Pete Best. EMI said he wasn't good enough. Ringo Starr was in bed at home when his mother announced that Brian Epstein was outside wanting to talk to him. In 1962 not everyone had a phone.

On 12 July 1962 the Rollin' Stones played their first show at the Marquee Club. Their eighteen-song set featured six tunes by Jimmy Reed. Ian Stewart said at the time that Mick, Keith and Brian were literally the only people in the UK at all familiar with this music. It's difficult to convey today just how far underground Chess rhythm and blues was in America at that time, let alone in the UK.

Fifteen-year-old David Jones was in a group called the Konrads, who played a few shows around Bromley in Kent. They made a single at Decca's studios in West Hampstead on 30 August 1962. He left soon after that because he wanted to play rhythm and blues, and changed his name to David Bowie.

Mick Jagger moved into a flat in Chelsea where he was joined by Keith Richards and Brian Jones. Jagger was still a student at the LSE at the time, though he wouldn't go back in September. He wasn't the only young person that summer trying to choose between higher education – just 4 per cent of eighteen-year-olds went to university in 1962 – and a future for which there was no template. In California, Al Jardine left the Beach Boys, who had already had a local hit with 'Surfin'', to go to college and study dentistry. In New York, Paul Simon was studying English Literature at Queens College while making demos for music publishers in his spare time.

In August 1962 Robert Zimmerman, who had already made a whole long-player, burned his boats and changed his name legally to Bob Dylan. With that name there was no way he was going home to Hibbing.

In July 1962 Andy Warhol unveiled his first one-man exhibition at the Ferus Gallery in Los Angeles. The exhibition consisted of thirty-two individual canvases of cans for different flavours of Campbell's soup. A young actor called Dennis Hopper bought one for $100.

In the summer of 1962 Joe Orton was serving his six-month sentence for defacing library books. Wilfrid Brambell, star of the BBC's comedy hit of the year *Steptoe and Son*, was arrested in a gentlemen's lavatory on Shepherd's Bush Green, not far from where his fictional character collected rags and bones.

In Jamaica, which became independent on 6 August 1962, the seventeen-year-old Bob Marley released his first record, a cover of a US country and western hit called 'One Cup Of Coffee', under the name Bobby Martell.

The communications satellite Telstar was launched on 10 July 1962. Within days producer Joe Meek had his Holloway Road studio working on the instrumental of the same name, which came out on 17 August. This was just two weeks after Marilyn Monroe had been found dead at the age of thirty-six.

Edward and Florence, the honeymoon couple in Ian McEwan's novel *On Chesil Beach*, dined in their hotel room in July 1962, possibly even on the same night the Rollin' Stones were playing Jimmy Reed at the Marquee, in 'an era when to be young was a social encumbrance, a mark of irrelevance, a faintly embarrassing condition for which marriage was the beginning of a cure'.

In the summer of 1962 nobody guessed youth was something you could prolong. The events of the coming winter, a cold one, would change all that. Not all the people who shivered through that winter, hatching plans for their own little careers, became as famous as the Beatles, the Rolling Stones, Andy Warhol, Bob Marley, Bob Dylan and Brian Wilson. Not all of them had a name which still resounds into the twenty-first century. Obviously there had to be a time when the rest of us hadn't heard of them. What's more amazing, given the way they and the sixties remain yoked together in the public imagination all these years later, is that there was ever a time when they hadn't heard of each other.

THE SECRET OF
'SATISFACTION'

On 6 May 1965 the Rolling Stones were on tour in Florida. Keith Richards woke up in the middle of the night in the Jack Tar Harrison Hotel in Clearwater with a riff going round in his head. He picked up his guitar, played the tune into his bedside tape recorder and went back to sleep. The following day he played it to Mick Jagger, who began thinking about some lyrics. Less than seven days later the band spent a day in RCA Studios in Hollywood recording three versions of the song. Six days after that they recorded the first public performance of the song for a TV show. By 27 May '(I Can't Get No) Satisfaction' was in the record shops in the UK. The US record company, being a tad slower, didn't manage to get it out until a week later.

If it's not actually the best record ever made, then 'Satisfaction' is as near as makes no difference. But here's the thing. It took just three weeks to pluck that feather of an idea from the depths of a dream, work it up into a song, build that up into a record and get it mixed, mastered, manufactured, marketed and messing with the heads of everyone on the planet with a pulse. Twenty-one days. There are no doubt people who will argue that had they had more time the Stones could have brought up the drums a little more and maybe dropped in some chick singers, polished up the second verse and generally improved it a little.

Hold it right there, put your hands above your head and step away from the mixing desk. 'Satisfaction' is beyond the reach of improvement. In fact, further performances and recordings of it have added not one whit to the itchy grandeur of the 1965 original. Stereo dissipates it. CD ruins it altogether. Live versions are either too fast or mask the rasping edge of that fuzz tone riff in a lather of over-amplification. Jagger has never sung it nearly as well again. I know this because I have just paid £5 on eBay to be reunited with the original mono version. I am here to tell you that Decca F12220 remains lightning in a bottle, a heart starter of a record, the tiny germ of genius that began the rock pandemic.

So, Rome may not have been built in a day but 'Satisfaction' was. And this in a world without motorways. When you had to book a transatlantic phone call. When television was in black and white. Before computers, mobile phones, fibre optics and the other paraphernalia that were supposed to accelerate the process of doing something and putting it out there. But don't.

Why? Because songwriting, recording, mixing, mulling over and the other preparation rituals all expand to fill the time available for them. Records are rarely made in small denominations like 'Satisfaction' any more. They emerge instead on albums, after elephantine periods of gestation. These are further prolonged by weeks of rewriting songs (that often should have been ditched in the first place), agonizing about producers, studios, equipment hire, the first single, the running order, the world tour, the video, and days in a hotel telling the world's media it's the best thing you've ever done. In rock there is a clear relationship between time taken and quality achieved. An inverse one. All this best practice is supposed to insure against failure. It doesn't.

In the days of 'Satisfaction' you were only as good as your next record. If 'Satisfaction' had flopped the Stones would have gone and invented another one and put that out six weeks later. The problem is nowadays you've spent all the money, the videos have already been shot, your media commitments have already been booked and you're going to be dragging this dead, reeking moose of a record around the pleasuredomes of the world for the next year or longer. You won't get to correct your mistakes for eighteen months.

There is no earthly sensible reason this should be so, particularly in the digital dispensation. We are supposed to be free of physical formats, aren't we? Arguably a band could dream up a song today, record it tomorrow and have it on the web in less than a week. Wouldn't that be a fine and a grand and a beautiful thing? So why won't it happen? Because the record business is saddled with an economic model which operates in its own interest rather than those of its customers, and bands have grown used to the amount of time it allows them to 'write the album'. This encourages farcical situations like the one Oasis found themselves in recently. They've shelved one album because they didn't like any of it. That must mean that there isn't one half-decent, salvageable note there. And these are the people who brought you *Be Here Now*.

If Oasis were focusing on putting all their energies into just one song and if that song was going to be available on the web next Friday they would be thinking differently. If they had a 'Live Forever' kicking about they would be desperate to share their secret with the greatest number of people as soon as possible. That's how Mick Jagger and Keith Richards felt back in 1965. As Dr Samuel Johnson would have said: 'Depend on it, sir. When a man knows he is to be hanged in a fortnight it concentrates his mind wonderfully.' And the good Doctor knew a thing or two about A&R.

THE GREATEST HOT STREAK IN POP

I n 2014 I interviewed Ray Davies at the Stratford Literary Festival. I wanted to know how he wrote all those great Kinks songs in the sixties. 'Some people wait for inspiration,' he said. 'I waited for a deadline.'

At the time the Kinks needed a new hit single roughly every three months, and Ray was the one who supplied them: 'You Really Got Me', 'All Day And All Of The Night', 'Tired Of Waiting For You', 'Ev'rybody's Gonna Be Happy', 'Set Me Free', 'See My Friends', 'Till The End Of The Day', 'Dedicated Follower Of Fashion', 'Sunny Afternoon', 'Dandy', 'Dead End Street', 'Waterloo Sunset', 'Autumn Almanac' and 'Days'.

That's fourteen smash hits in four years. My friend Mark Ellen's fond of describing it as the greatest hot streak in the history of pop. It's even more amazing when you consider they were all written and sung by one person. Ray wasn't sharing the responsibility with John or Paul or Mick or Keith. That's what you call pressure, and judging by the outcome pressure appears to be every bit as effective as inspiration.

There's one further single which sometimes gets forgotten in that sequence and it was raised by somebody in the audience at Stratford. 'Wonderboy' came out in the spring of 1968 and stalled at number thirty-six, which was disappointing by Kinks standards. Davies draws comfort from the fact that somebody told him that John Lennon loved it, demanding it was played three times in a row by a DJ in a club because he liked the middle eight so much. That may be an apocryphal tale but if it was my song I too would do my best to keep it alive.

CATCHING UP WITH BOB DYLAN

first heard the sound of Bob Dylan on a school-owned wood-panelled record player at an after-lessons folk club in 1963. I'd heard his songs done by people like Peter, Paul & Mary but had never been exposed to the experience of hearing him sing. I still thought you pronounced his name Dye-lon – an indication of how likely you were to hear him on the radio at the time and also how familiar we were with poetry.

I remember it was a shock but an exciting one. It was a voice that seemed to contain multitudes, from rhythm and blues to the cowboy music we'd grown up liking as kids. In the fifty years since that time I've blown hot and cold over Dylan but he's always retained his fascination and I've never changed in my belief that he is a brilliant singer. He may not have much of a voice but he's a brilliant singer in that I can't think of anything he's done, whether it's 'The Times They Are A-Changin" or 'Must Be Santa', that doesn't in some way ring true.

I've never been one of those people who feel the need to attend every show by anybody. Musical acts aren't like football teams. They don't depend on your support. If you don't go somebody else will. In fact, particularly with people like Bob Dylan and Bruce Springsteen, my view is that old fans should stand aside and let the youngsters go, if they want, because at least they'll be seeing something the like of which they have never seen before and probably will never see again. However, in November 2013, on the fiftieth anniversary of my first exposure to Bob Dylan, I got the offer of a ticket to see him at the Albert Hall.

I hadn't planned to go. My old friend Nick Stewart very kindly invited me. I couldn't believe how close we were. Row 1, seats 108 and 109. Go and look at the seating plan to see how close we were. We reckoned we were about twenty feet away from the microphone. Actually it was more like fifteen when he played the piano and as little as twelve when he came and took a drink between numbers.

You don't get many opportunities to observe a legend at close quarters for a couple of hours. All the lights are behind him, discouraging any examination of his features. When he walks he bounces, like a puppet whose head is slightly too big for his body. When he comes to the microphone to sing he holds on to it like a politician addressing farmers somewhere on the prairie.

He looks as if he belongs to a flyover state rather than Los Angeles or New York. He's wearing a Nudie-type suit with powder blue panels. His band are dressed in grey suits and black shirts. It could have been a county fair. When he wants to emphasize a lyric he puts his hand to his hip in a manner reminiscent of Larry Grayson. There's an odd tentativeness about him since he abandoned the guitar, as if he's looking around for a new crutch.

He plays hardly any old. I would have been happy if he hadn't played any. Most of the songs come from *Tempest* or one of the albums immediately before it. He narrates the songs rather than sings them but the band definitely play them, and play them well. You can see all five of them watching him closely at all times, clearly aware that he could do anything without warning.

It was intense, particularly on 'High Water', 'Scarlet Town' and 'Long And Wasted Years', but despite that intensity he didn't seem to use up any of himself. He found a new way to keep going in the mid-eighties. John le Carré said he wasn't doing any more interviews because he couldn't afford 'the expense of soul' it involved. Bob Dylan seems to have avoided that problem. I stood there and looked at him and thought, 'I've been watching and listening to you for fifty years now and still you give nothing away. It's this that keeps me coming back. There's a lesson there. It's not what you give; it's what you withhold.'

WHY SIXTIES ROCK STARS NEVER GIVE UP

A few years ago I was talking to Ron Wood of the Rolling Stones. At that stage Ron was well into the fourth decade of a career in music, a career that had begun in the mid-sixties with the Birds. He remembered that when, back in the sixties, he told his mother he was going to quit his studies and join a band she had warned him that this wasn't a job that would last and he would be better off doing what his classmates had done. Studying hard. Getting a qualification. The sort that leads to a steady job with a good pension.

Well, clearly he didn't do that, but what, I wondered, happened to all the classmates who did? They were, of course, shunted into early retirement in middle age. Either that or their jobs had been rendered redundant by the march of time and technology. But there was no such redundancy for the veteran plank spanker. The job that was supposed to have the life expectancy of a mayfly had turned out to be the best bet of all.

You couldn't honestly say that age had not withered Ron, and custom was never called upon to stale his infinite variety because he never had a lot of variety in the first place. Ron essentially still does what Ron did at the age of twenty, just a lot more profitably. Since our conversation Ron has gone on to enter his fifth decade as a rock and roller and most recently provided proof of that happy breed's refusal to yield to Anno Domini by fathering twins at the age of almost seventy.

In October this year he and the rest of the Rolling Stones will be headlining one of the shows at a special festival in the Californian desert. Their support act will be Bob Dylan, who has recently turned seventy-five. Paul McCartney, Neil Young, the Who and Roger Waters of Pink Floyd will also be represented. The demand for tickets for the first weekend was so great that they added a further weekend. The enduring appeal of veterans like these is now so commonplace that nobody has bothered to perform the old sub-editor's trick of calculating the combined ages of the musicians on stage because they would undoubtedly run out of fingers.

Even within the Stones organization this latest payday is now airily referred to as the 'catch 'em before they croak' festival. Even the bands look upon this unsought longevity with wry bemusement. It is a situation rich in irony. The generation who said they hoped they died before they got old are now setting standards for long service which no previous generation of musicians could match. Frank Sinatra initially retired at the age of fifty-six because he didn't feel you could be a convincing crooner beyond that age.

The members of U2 are currently sailing past the age at which the Chairmen of the Board retired and there seems no reason why they should stop upon reaching sixty, seventy, or even – is it possible? – eighty.

For those who can remember when Mick Jagger used to give interviews saying, 'I can't imagine doing this when I'm forty' there is a certain grim amusement in seeing his giant wrinkly face filling the outdoor screens in front of crowds who are numbered in the tens, even hundreds, of thousands. That giant image can be frightening. As George Melly said, 'Those can't be laughter lines – nothing's that funny.'

However, there's no point trying to speculate when, if ever, the Rolling Stones will call it a day. Their continuing popularity makes a mockery of such speculation. And we really should know better than to ask the question we so often ask, which is usually some variation on a theme of 'Why do they keep on doing it? They can't need the money.'

Let's deal with the money first. Many of us keep on working long after the requirements of food and shelter have been taken care of. Everybody wants to get some more money and that includes the people who've already got quite a lot. Plus they're the people with the outgoings which have to be paid for. Nobody says to Sir Philip Green or Richard Branson, 'Haven't you got enough money?' So why do we feel justified making the same point to Bob Dylan? Is it because we don't think he ought to be interested in money?

Rock stars often aren't very good with money or particularly conversant with the details of it, but they are certainly interested in having a lot of it and not just because they want to buy more houses and jewels. They're interested in it for the simple reason that it's the most reliable measure of where they stand in the affections of the public and in relation to each other. Although they affect a hippy disinterest in vulgar status, the minute they hear that one of their peers from the *Sunday Night at the London Palladium* roundabout has earned a record sum for playing on some undreamt-of scale they call in their advisers and demand to know why they haven't been offered at least as much and preferably more. And if you're one of those acts playing the festival in the desert, who all made their bones in the sixties and seventies, your bargaining hand is strengthened by the fact that you're a commodity, like land, that they simply aren't making any more of. Promoters or sponsors will sign a cheque for Paul McCartney that they will never sign for, say, Taylor Swift. They're both musicians, but only one is living history.

And nowadays, no matter who they are, these people have to go out to earn money. It no longer comes to them. There was a time when a handful of musicians could stay at home and live off the revenue stream from record sales. That hasn't been the case for more than ten years, since the market for so-called physical product died. This is why everybody, from the newest acts to the most venerable ones, is now on the road all the time.

When Leonard Cohen's business manager embezzled over ten million dollars from him he responded by going back on the road even though he was seventy-three at the time. To his delighted surprise he found himself playing bigger venues than ever before, for fans who ranged in age from his original sixties followers to their grandchildren, all of whom were paying the best part of £50 to be in his presence. Touring proved to be so lucrative he continued doing it for years, one tour merging into another until he was almost matching Bob Dylan, who claims that he's on a 'never-ending tour'.

This is not something you can dabble in. If you're going to play live for a long period of time then you need to get yourself high-quality musicians. They don't come cheap, and if they're going to dedicate themselves to you, you have to guarantee them a certain amount of work. The decision of whether to tour or not doesn't just involve you. It's a decision which has knock-on effects for the mortgages and child support payments and health insurance plans of whole teams of people. Many's the band who have lined up a number of festival appearances for this summer to top up the pension plans of a bunch of already affluent seniors. These musicians are very fortunate that they can earn sums of money in their sixties which were not available to them when they were thirty and, ironically, at their best. And this doesn't just apply to the musicians on stage. It also applies to the people who build the stage, tune the guitars, run the lights, provide the catering and do the accounts. If you're a rock star, all these people are your dependents. If you don't work, they don't work.

Then there are the family members. When these rock stars first made some money the only family members they had to share it with were their parents, who were usually grateful to have a nice bungalow to move into. Forty years later they have dependent relatives as far as the eye can see. There may be some ex-wives. There will certainly be children who have found that growing up as the son or daughter of a rock and roll legend has left them unsuited to normal employment and therefore they will have been found some niche in the retinue. They may be helping out in wardrobe, shooting video backstage, doing on-tour logistics and even, in an increasing number of cases, joining the band in some position where any shortcomings they might have are not too badly exposed. All these people have to be paid for and none of them work for the minimum wage. They have grown up amid wealth and status and expect to be kept in the style to which they have become accustomed.

When Bob Dylan came to England to play the Isle of Wight Festival in 1969 he gave a press conference. One of the questions he was asked was why he'd come to the Isle of Wight. His answer was that he wanted to see the home of Alfred Lord Tennyson. I like to think that he came up with that answer because he couldn't believe that the question had been put. Nobody asks the oil rig worker why he's come to visit the North Sea. Nobody expects the international businessman to explain what personal foible has led him to Frankfurt. Nobody asks a roofer what he's doing on the roof. Being a rock star is, like anything else, a job of work, and like most workers rock stars will go wherever the best-paid, most congenial, most rewarding work is. That's what took Bob Dylan to the Isle of Wight. It's the same thing that will take you to your job on Monday. Money.

It says a lot about our childlike illusions that we find it hard to accept that rock stars do anything for money. In this we are not prepared to extend to them the same slack we permit ourselves. We can just about accept that great artists such as Dickens and Shakespeare were interested in the fiscal side of life. We know that movie stars get paid insane sums to feature in blockbusters. And yet the news that a much-loved rock performer might be playing some major festival this summer and he and his operation will be turning over a million pounds in the course of a few hours' work is something that we take as a personal affront. We see rock stars as being above petty concerns of money and career. Here is the news. They're not. Nor are we. They work for the same reasons we do.

The clinching reason why rock musicians continue to insert their sixty- and seventy-year-old bodies into the sort of clothes which were decided for them when they were in their early thirties, the reason they put themselves through gruelling fitness regimes in order to be able to drop to their knees in the shadow of the microphone stand at an age when most of their contemporaries are having hips and knees replaced, the reason they stay up long past their bedtimes to sing songs about being young and ready to go all night, is because they can.

Sixty-year-old former football stars want nothing more than to pull on the strip and turn out for their old team this Saturday but they know it's not possible and instead they've had to settle for a life which is a long rest after a brief period of exertion, a period which they didn't appreciate sufficiently at the time. They have spent most of their lives slowly absorbing the lesson that you're a long time retired.

But rock stars don't have to retire. If you could go on stage tonight and people would ask nothing more than that you repeat a bunch of songs and moves which you first did at the age of twenty-eight, in exchange for which you're guaranteed the full-throated approval of tens of thousands of people, many of them less than half your age – a transporting experience which is the emotional equivalent of scoring a goal in a World Cup final every night; if you could have the feeling of power that comes from being able to get herds of people to do this when you point this way, and do that when you point the other way, and at the end of the day you're going to get paid more than most people make in a year, I venture to suggest that you would do it.

And you would do it repeatedly. After a while you would have to admit to yourself that you were addicted to that feeling. This, ultimately, is the reason why everybody else retires but rock stars never do. It's because as they stand there centre stage, listening to the band churning through some well-worn favourite behind them, watching the sea of bobbing heads that stretch to the horizon, and knowing exactly which number they're going to do next and how the crowd will react, they realize the terrible secret that they dare not share with their nearest and dearest. They have come to realize that nothing else that life has to offer – not a wedding day or the birth of a child, not a heady promotion at work or the thrill of a job well done, none of the things that ordinary people dream of – can offer the thrilling validation that is available to them every night. Nothing else in their life comes close. That's why they keep doing it. And that's why they will keep doing it until their very last breath.

THE OTHER SIDE OF
THE SIXTIES

Although the B-side of a single earns almost as much for the performer and writer as the A-side does, it's the fact that nobody seems to have anything riding on it that earns it a special place in the hearts of those whose love of pop music is not satisfied by mere radio play. In the sixties true fans knew as much about the B-side as they did about the A- or plug side, largely because they owned it, and they also loved it for the different light it threw on the pop process.

The B-side could be where people got to show off a side of themselves the wider audience might not have been familiar with: it still beggars belief that Paul McCartney's Little Richard knock-off 'I'm Down' was cut the same day he did 'Yesterday'. Similarly, on the other side of 'Holiday', here are the Bee Gees showing us the Goths they would have been if given half a chance; and the

Everlys, venting their spite on the obverse of the wobbly lipped 'Crying In The Rain'.

There were some recordings that everybody thought were just too damn obvious to be on the A-side, records that were subsequently turned over by posterity. Here you have the likes of Them's 'Gloria', which was on the other side of the memorable 'Baby, Please Don't Go', and Arthur Alexander's imperishable anthem 'A Shot Of Rhythm And Blues', which was first pushed out on the B-side of the comparatively modest 'You Better Move On'.

There were songs that were ahead of their time – Marianne Faithfull's 'Sister Morphine' was put out as a B-side in 1969 and then hurriedly withdrawn, fully two years before the Rolling Stones' version came out. Marvin Gaye's original of 'Wherever I Lay My Hat (That's My Home)' was the B-side of a 1969 single fourteen years before it became a huge worldwide hit for Paul Young. And so on.

Anyway, this is a list of fifty of my favourite B-sides from the sixties, because the sixties was the decade of the B-side. It includes a few, such as the Byrds' 'I'll Feel A Whole Lot Better', that are better than the plug sides; the odd one, such as the Bonzos' flip of 'I'm The Urban Spaceman', which I include for sentimental or capricious reasons; and a few epics, like the Righteous Brothers' 'Unchained Melody' and the Band's 'The Night They Drove Old Dixie Down', which you can't believe any sentient being ever thought could tolerate being on the other side of anything.

I remember a coffee bar from my teenage years. It was called the Shady Nook, largely because there was a tree mysteriously growing out of the centre of the table in the back of the place. More to the point there was a jukebox. Here we schoolkids would linger over warm Coke or milky coffee from clear cups, pooling our coins to play as many of our favourite B-sides as we could. You got three plays for a shilling. Make your choice.

The Beach Boys: 'Wendy' ('Good Vibrations')

The Beatles: 'I'm Down' ('Help!')

The Rolling Stones: 'Off The Hook' ('Little Red Rooster')

The Animals: 'Club A Gogo' ('Don't Let Me Be Misunderstood')

The Byrds: 'I'll Feel A Whole Lot Better' ('All I Really Want To Do')

Arthur Alexander: 'A Shot Of Rhythm And Blues' (You Better Move On)

Them: 'Gloria' ('Baby, Please Don't Go')

Bob Dylan: 'From A Buick 6' ('Positively 4th Street')

The Bee Gees: 'Every Christian Lion Hearted Man Will Show You' ('Holiday')

The Bonzo Dog Band: 'Canyons Of Your Mind' ('I'm The Urban Spaceman')

David Bowie: 'The London Boys' ('Rubber Band')

The Kinks: 'I'm Not Like Everybody Else' ('Sunny Afternoon')

The Who: 'Circles' ('Substitute')

The Small Faces: 'Just Passing' ('I Can't Make It')

Gerry and the Pacemakers: 'You'll Never Walk Alone' ('How Do You Do It?')

Nancy Sinatra: 'Summer Wine' ('Sugar Town')

Lulu: 'The Boat That I Row' ('To Sir With Love')

The McCoys: 'Sorrow' ('Fever')

Roy Orbison: 'Love Hurts' ('Running Scared')

Simon & Garfunkel: 'For Emily, Whenever I May Find Her' ('A Hazy Shade Of Winter')

Otis Redding: 'Down In The Valley' ('My Girl')

Marvin Gaye: 'Wherever I Lay My Hat (That's My Home)' ('Too Busy Thinking About My Baby')

Dusty Springfield: 'My Colouring Book' ('I Just Don't Know What To Do With Myself')

Cream: 'Tales Of Brave Ulysses' ('Strange Brew')

The Everly Brothers: 'I'm Not Angry' ('Crying In The Rain')

The Troggs: 'From Home' ('Wild Thing')

Jimi Hendrix Experience: 'The Wind Cries Mary' ('Purple Haze')

The Band: 'The Night They Drove Old Dixie Down' ('Up On Cripple Creek')

Creedence Clearwater Revival: 'Born On The Bayou' ('Proud Mary')

Elvis Presley: 'A Mess Of Blues' ('It's Now Or Never')

The Mamas and Papas: 'Got A Feelin'' ('Monday Monday')

The Temptations: 'Don't Look Back' ('My Baby')

Neil Young: 'Sugar Mountain' ('The Loner')

Stevie Wonder: 'I Don't Know Why' ('My Cherie Amour')

Smokey Robinson and the Miracles: 'Choosey Beggar' ('Going To A Go-Go')

The Lovin' Spoonful: 'Didn't Want To Have To Do It' ('Did You Ever Have To Make Up Your Mind?')

The Righteous Brothers: 'Unchained Melody' ('Hung On You')

Procol Harum: 'Good Captain Clack' ('Homburg')

Yes: 'Something's Coming' ('Yours Is No Disgrace')

Traffic: 'Coloured Rain' ('Here We Go Round The Mulberry Bush')

Harpers Bizarre: 'Witchi Tai To' ('Knock On Wood')

The Turtles: 'We'll Meet Again' ('Happy Together')

Marianne Faithfull: 'Sister Morphine' ('Something Better')

Jeff Beck: 'Beck's Bolero' ('Hi Ho Silver Lining')

Sam Cooke: 'A Change Is Gonna Come' ('Shake')

Scott Walker: 'My Death' ('Mathilde')

Led Zeppelin: 'Communication Breakdown' ('Good Times Bad Times')

Incredible String Band: 'No Sleep Blues' ('Painting Box')

Donovan: 'To Sing For You' ('Colours')

The Doors: 'Love Street' ('Hello, I Love You')

3
CREDIBILITY GAPS –
THE RADIO 3 ESSAYS

Frank Zappa famously said, 'Writing about music is like tap dancing about architecture.' I think he had a point. Music is beyond words. That's what it's there for.

How, then, have I managed to spend most of my professional life writing about rock music and the people who make it? In plenty of cases I've done the same as most of the people who write about music, which is to avoid talking about the music wherever possible and writing instead about all the things that surround it.

Here the professionals are no different from the public. If you ask people whether they like a piece of music they justify their liking by saying how much they admire the performer. If they don't like it they reach for observations such as 'it's overproduced' because they think that makes them sound analytical.

People are uncomfortable saying, 'I just like it.' If they like something they like to think they can justify their liking. They're a lot happier if the person making the music they like seems somehow worthy of their admiration. In the world of classical music this traditionally meant they were some kind of virtuoso. That's not so easy with pop.

In pop, the quality that replaced virtuosity was credibility. In fact pop music's the only area of the arts where the adjective 'credible' is in daily use. What exactly does that mean? Can we believe them? Can we believe in them? Are they real? Are they telling us the truth? Are they only in it for the money or the fame? Are they pure in heart?

If there's one thing I've learned about rock stars it's that none of them come to their work with motivations less than, let's say, mixed. There's very little pure about what they do. They do what they do for money, for glory, to get back at the competition, because they find it exciting and, most crowningly, because this is what they do. If they're like most performing artists the thought actually going through their heads when they're on stage is most likely to be 'I can't believe I'm getting away with this'.

We're the ones who make credibility such a big deal when we're thinking about pop music. I wrote about this in a series of talks for BBC Radio 3's programme *The Essay* in 2017. It's one of the few places on the airwaves where you can talk about a theme like this rather than about somebody's latest record or whether Bob Dylan should have got the Nobel Prize, and I thank them for the opportunity.

NOTHING IS REAL . . .
LEAST OF ALL ROCK

It's fifty years since John Lennon wrote 'Strawberry Fields Forever'. The song took its name from a children's home he remembered from his days growing up in Liverpool. But in truth it's not about the children's home. Like a lot of the Beatles' greatest records, like a lot of great pop records, it's not about anything so much as the emotional state John Lennon was going through when he wrote it. John had taken LSD. This had led him to conclude that real life was a dream and the real truth was however he happened to be feeling. The key line of the song, the one that rings down the years, is 'nothing is real'.

In these essays I want to look at pop music's obsession with what's real and what's not, with what's authentic and what just sounds as though it's authentic, and the whole complex, often contradictory business of how some people get to be regarded as 'credible' while others are not.

I'm not one of those people here to tell you that this is the new classical music. I don't believe that. As soon as people start talking about pop music as though it's Stravinsky they immediately take away half of what I like about it: they take away the personality, the pretension, the absurdity, the constant battle between career and ego and art (with a small 'a'). As soon as you approach pop music with a furrowed brow it flees. Ever since the heavy papers started covering it people have worried about pop far too much. I come from a different point of view. Pope John Paul II said, 'Of all the unimportant things football is the most important.' I feel the same way about pop music.

What interests me is what our struggles with it tell us about ourselves. I'm fascinated by the contortions we get ourselves into when trying to justify and validate the simple pleasure we get from the music. If we like something we apparently have to find a way to prove that it is more worth our while than the things we like less. One of the ways we do this is by deciding whether it is or is not real. This has particularly dogged popular music ever since the Beatles.

One of the key ways in which pop differs most sharply from classical music is that the personality and background of the people performing the music are as important as the music itself. This didn't begin with the Beatles. I trace it back to John Lomax. Lomax was born in Mississippi just after the American Civil War. During the 1920s and 1930s he made his living on the borders between academia and showmanship. Radio had just become widespread and there was a feeling that the old music, which was somehow deemed authentic because it was old, was in danger of being driven out by this new music, which couldn't possibly be authentic because it was new. Lomax set himself the job of journeying out into rural America and finding the people who still sang the old songs, or even better made up songs themselves. These would ideally be people whose experience was not tainted by exposure to mass media or the conventions of polite society.

On one of these field trips, to the fearsome Angola Penitentiary in Louisiana, he found and recorded Huddie Ledbetter, who was serving time for murder. Ledbetter was an imposing man who had acquired the name 'Lead Belly'. Lead Belly knew lots of songs, from children's favourites to Broadway show tunes, but Lomax was mainly interested in the kind of songs that might be plausibly sung by a guy with the name Lead Belly. These would be songs about suffering, privation, violence and death.

John Lomax knew what his audience, who considered themselves sophisticated, were looking for. There is nobody so easy to fool as the person who thinks he knows something and the audiences for Lomax's field recordings, who were predominantly academics and leftists, had an appetite for hearing about suffering. Whereas the wealthy tourists going to the Cotton Club in Harlem might have preferred to be entertained by happy-appearing negroes, the people at Lomax's illustrated lectures in university towns wanted to hear about misery, and Lomax was happy to provide it.

Musical accounts of suffering were his stock in trade. In 1940 he cornered the Georgia street singer Blind Willie McTell in a hotel room in Atlanta and got him to play almost all his repertoire. The conversations between songs were picked up on the recording and are very illuminating. What Lomax keeps nagging Willie for is what he calls 'complaining songs', particularly songs complaining about how the white man treats the negro. Blind Willie McTell pretends not to know what he's talking about and instead plays him his new one, a perky tune in praise of romantic love called 'King Edward Blues', which was inspired by the abdication of the English throne. You feel for Lomax. He's come looking for reality and the grittier the better. Instead he gets *Hello!* magazine.

When Lead Belly made his first East Coast appearance in front of an audience of a thousand academics in evening dress, Lomax winced when he saw him pass the hat around afterwards. 'Smacked of sensationalism,' he huffed. However, he and Lead Belly both profited from the promotion of the personality of the singer being billed by the newspapers as 'the sweet singer of the swamplands here to do a few tunes between homicides'. This is what they call in the days of TV talent shows 'the backstory'.

Lead Belly was a pioneer of what we might call unpopular music. That is, music that's simple and catchy but doesn't actually command a large audience. They didn't care for Lead Belly up in Harlem so he confined himself to playing for prosperous white audiences. He attached himself to Lomax as driver, guide, ambassador and demonstrator of material. This is how he came to be appearing with him on stage from time to time wearing convicts' stripes or the bib and braces of a farmhand, even though in real life he favoured double-breasted three-piece suits much as Jimmy Cagney would have worn. In this he was merely meeting audience expectations. The further an audience is removed from the reality of the working life the more they like to feel that they are being entertained by somebody who has actually lived that life.

Twenty years after Lead Belly came to New York a university

dropout called Robert Zimmerman arrived in the same city to make a name for himself as a folk singer. The name he chose was Bob Dylan, not for Dylan Thomas but for the character Matt Dillon in the Western TV series *Gunsmoke*. He told the people in the big city that he'd run away with the circus as a child, that he'd hopped freight trains, that he'd learned how to play the guitar from an old bluesman called Wigglefoot. It was all entirely made up, every last bit of it, but the people he told it to didn't query it because they badly wanted to believe it was real. They wanted to believe it because believing in Bob Dylan made his performance of old folk songs easier to believe in. As Joni Mitchell pointed out almost fifty years later, 'Bobby invented a character to deliver his songs.' In fact I would argue that Dylan's single most creative act was to invent Bob Dylan and then to remain behind that mask, never once letting it slip, for over fifty years.

When I saw him a few years back at the Albert Hall he did one of the most remarkable bits of business I've ever seen on the rock stage. When it came time for the curtain call he and his band lined up centre stage. They had their hands at their sides like cowboys making ready to draw. They didn't touch each other or smile at us. They just looked out at the audience for a full minute and then, obeying some unseen and unheard signal, the tableau broke up and they left the stage. It struck me that, despite the complete absence of pyrotechnics, smart lighting and obvious staging, this was one of the most theatrical things I'd ever seen on a rock stage. Far more convincingly theatrical than, for instance, David Bowie. It could only have happened the way it did because somebody, presumably Bob Dylan, planned it that way. Was it real? It was about as real as a musical number in a Busby Berkeley movie.

We make a lot of those pop acts who go in for obviously theatrical presentation. In fact the most theatrical acts are the ones who don't appear theatrical at all. The Pet Shop Boys often perform in masks and surround themselves with dancers. Does that make them any more or less theatrical than, say, U2, whose entire act is a celebration of ordinariness on a massive scale? Probably not. The set of *Look Back in Anger* is every bit as much an artifice as the set of *Aida*. Bruce Springsteen's act is no more real than Beyoncé's. It's all to do with expectations. Springsteen's audience wouldn't like it if he came on dressed in an expensive suit. Beyoncé's audience wouldn't like it if she came on in denim and leather. The difference between the two audiences is that Beyoncé's know they're seeing a show whereas Springsteen's think they're seeing something somehow more real.

Nothing in this business is real. The theatrics in pop don't begin when the lights go down. Keith Richards is Keith Richards twenty-four hours a day. That's why he's endured. The gravel-voiced boozer polymath character that we know as Tom Waits was developed by young Thomas Waits while working as a doorman at a California club. He was so good at entertaining the crowd that some nights there were more people outside the club than inside. This was method acting on a full-time basis. It was only by building the Tom Waits character that he could then get away with writing the kind of songs that Tom Waits would sing.

Most recently the artist known as Seasick Steve, who appeared as if out of nowhere on BBC TV in 2006 and claimed to have spent most of his sixty-plus years as a hobo bluesman, was revealed to have actually spent most of his career doing what jobbing musicians do, which is playing wherever somebody will pay, even if that means performing middling disco records, the sort that hobo bluesmen are reckoned to have little truck with. Will it affect his career? That probably depends on how good his material is.

People like Springsteen and Waits have reached a workable compromise between the people they are and the people that other people pay to see them act out on stage. Their artistry isn't confined to their songs. It extends to their persona as well. They know what they would do and what they wouldn't. John Lennon, who sang 'nothing is real', never got the chance to work that out for himself. He was the person who called himself the working-class hero, which is something he certainly wasn't. Like Bruce Springsteen and Bob Dylan he had made sure that he knew as little as possible about the working life.

Other people find it harder to draw the line. Richey Edwards of the Welsh punk group the Manic Street Preachers was challenged by a journalist to prove how much he lived out the music he played. So he took out a knife and carved the words 'for real' in his arm. One of the reasons Kurt Cobain of Nirvana killed himself in 1994 was that he felt bad about making many millions of dollars doing something he would happily have done for free.

Cobain's last performance was a recording of the show *Unplugged* for MTV. *Unplugged* was the pinnacle of rock's affair with authenticity. Here the hit acts were encouraged to do away with their amplification and special effects and just perch on stools and play, as if in this act of stripping away the performer would reveal his real self. Cobain finished with a song by Lead Belly. It was the best performance he ever did.

WHY DOES POP NEED SO MANY NAMES?

One of the things that makes classical music classical is there's an agreed way of describing it. When *The Grove Dictionary of Music and Musicians* says 'classical' means 'any music that does not belong to folk or popular traditions and is regarded as a model of excellence or formal discipline' there can't be many who would disagree. Similarly with a historical term like 'baroque' – 'European music 1600 to 1750' – and even a technical one like 'minimal' – 'static harmony, patterned rhythms and repetition' – there's a crisp certainty about how the musical map is divided.

This is not the way things work in post-Elvis Presley popular music. Here things aren't organized at all. There's no *Grove*. If there were it would be bursting at the seams, such is the energy that pop music puts into giving names to the sub-varieties it is forever spawning. Sixty years after Presley it's more complex than ever. For instance once there was dance music, which wasn't the same as music for dancing, and then there was trance music which begat acid trance, Balearic trance, hard trance, psychedelic trance, progressive trance, techno trance, vocal trance and so on ad infinitum.

Much as George Bernard Shaw said it was impossible for one Englishman to open his mouth without making another Englishman hate him, genre terms are the elevator heels of musical taxonomy, enabling one alleged music lover to achieve their key objective, which is to gain enough height to be able to look down on another music lover.

It didn't begin like this. In the beginning there was rock and roll, which should be a simple enough idea to grasp. Like many of the most useful terms that have been employed to map popular music – jazz and funk for instance – it was originally African-American code for sex.

Rock ampersand roll indicates something different from the two words separated by a couple of apostrophes and the orphaned letter 'n'. The latter contraction – said as 'rock'n'roll' – denotes something in the tradition of Jerry Lee Lewis. In its longer ampersand form it means something more self-important.

Back in the day when most people bought their records from Boots and Smith's everything would be filed together under 'pop'. Then at some point in the late sixties this was changed to 'pop' and 'rock'. Then in the early seventies it was decided there had to be a further form of apartheid which should keep the purveyors of pop records, which were mainly bought by girls, away from the high priests of rock, whose records were mainly bought by boys.

The pop/rock split is the Sunni/Shia schism of popular music. It is the original sin of snobbery from which all subsequent snobberies descend. The theory is as follows: pop acts are interested in hit singles, and therefore they value catchy tunes and sentiments with which larger audiences can identify; rock acts, on the other hand, are primarily motivated by the desire to fulfil their artistic mission. However, even the most superficial inspection of what actually happens shows that rock acts value hit singles every bit as much as anybody else, but simply don't like to be seen to be working too hard at achieving them.

The term 'pop music' summons up pictures of Abba, of the Spice Girls, of bright shiny entertainment shows and elaborate dance routines. The term 'rock music' conjures pictures of unshaven men grimacing over their fretboards with that 'I suffered for my art, now it's your turn' look on their faces. Pop music is about pleasure. Rock music is about, or at least allegedly about, worth, substance and – don't laugh – gravitas. There is a tendency among some people even to use the expression 'just pop music'. As if pop music was something a serious musician could shrug off without thinking. That isn't the case. A weighty musician is no better equipped to produce a pop soufflé than a prima ballerina is to dance like Ginger Rogers.

Pop success is, if anything, more enduring than rock credibility because it is more to do with the music than the people who play it. To have a hit single you need to appeal to people who like the music. To have a hit album you need to appeal to people who like you. That might account for the decline in the number of old-fashioned rock stars in the years since the single track download and the musical stream supplanted the album.

It has been my experience over the years that there is a fundamental difference between the way young women respond to music and the way young men respond to music. When hearing a piece of music in a public place the female of the species will tend to say, 'I like this, what is it?' A male on the other hand will first of all find out who is performing the music and only then, having run down his mental list of the things his self-image allows him to like, will he tell you whether he likes it or not.

There is a memorable scene in the 1982 film *Diner* in which Daniel Stern's character, a painfully serious collector of records, finds his wife (Ellen Barkin) has not put them back in the right sections. When he finds James Brown has been filed with the rock and roll records he almost bursts into tears. In his world the classification of music is almost as important as listening to it. 'This is important to me,' he pleads, struggling to keep his emotions in check.

There is a massive racial component to all this classification. There always has been. Nowadays they call it 'urban' but it was once 'rhythm and blues' and before that 'race music'. In ten years' time it will be some other euphemism which will be advanced by somebody seeking to make their name. This process never stops. As soon as a variety of music has a name then some enterprising taste maker can position himself as the person who provides this variety and will seek to persuade a radio station that they really ought to be finding a place on their schedules for it.

In the early seventies, pop, rock and soul were joined by something called 'progressive', which was the harbinger of the holier-than-thou approach to musical classification. Progressive meant 'made by the whitest people you've ever seen'. Then there was punk, which was made by people who knew two chords, wore leather jackets and didn't need your stinking money. This was soon softened into 'new wave', which meant people who had leather jackets but wanted as much of your stinking money as you cared to give them.

Then somebody invented indie rock, which was a category that welcomed all those thousands of people who felt their music was too fine and piercingly sincere to permit it being bought by anyone other than people who felt the same way about it as the people who made it. They adopted this name initially because they were signed not by the major record companies, but by the independents. That didn't last long. What started out as a way of referring to the way the music was distributed eventually turned into a term supposed to characterize how the music sounded. 'Indie'.

That wasn't the end of it. Oh no. Sometimes it seems the key measure of the indie rock movement has been not so much the talent it has thrown up as the unprecedented contribution it has made to the bewildering splintering of popular music. Punk, post-punk, alt rock, alt country, shoe gaze, paisley underground, psych, hard core, grind core, thrash metal, Nintendocore, sludge metal, doom metal, death metal, metal metal. As you wend your way into the darkness the terms turn uglier and more challenging, seeming to say, 'Are you sure you have the stomach to follow this music this far?' This is music that is fiercely, proudly unpopular and constantly in the business of inventing unlovely new descriptors to ensure it stays that way. Each one is like a roughly painted sign hammered on top of a wall topped with barbed wire. The overarching message is, beyond this wall are people who have driven to the very core of the particular thing they happen to like and who are consequently more real than you could possibly imagine.

They are also descriptors that are primarily for the benefit of the people making the music and for the narrow group of people who like it. This is what the makers of the film *This Is Spinal Tap* meant when they had the manager of the fictional band say, 'It's not that we're less popular. It's just that our appeal is getting more selective.'

Most of these terms seem tired to me, not only because so many have hung on long after the moment is passed. Anybody who sits on a stool and sings to the accompaniment of their own acoustic guitar is allowed to be 'folk' even though they cooked up their songs while on a mixed media course at some college and have never met any actual folk in their lives. All music which is sung in another language is now classified as 'world music' and as such granted a kind of presumed authentic status, like necklaces of beads sold to tourists on foreign beaches. Anything done by a white American that mentions a city or a highway is swept up as Americana, a term invented to reflect the fact that the people who liked country music didn't like the idea of country music. Even though the Rolling Stones made their name on their ability to make records that people danced to, nobody would dream of allowing them to be played on a dance radio programme because nowadays 'dance' means highly stylized music using electronic instruments, the kind that is played in clubs.

I would like to advance a solution. I propose a sweeping away of all this surplus nomenclature and its replacement by one simple term. There is only one term that holds good from sea to shining sea, that applies just as perfectly to the high-sheen products of the

Taylor Swift factory as it does to the latest record by Kasabian, that covers grime as well as Led Zeppelin, and under whose welcoming shingles you can shelter the Beatles as well as Kanye West, and that is the term that was in wide use at the beginning of the 1960s. In those days they called it all 'beat music'. That still works for me. The beat is the thing they have in common. The beat is the primal pulse we all respond to.

LOUDNESS IS THE POINT

In 1992 the Brit Awards took place at the Hammersmith Odeon. As I took my seat that night I noticed I was just a few rows behind the great conductor Sir Georg Solti and his party. They were on hand to pick up the award for his recording of Verdi's *Otello*.

Representatives of the classical fraternity are an awkward presence at the Brit Awards, which is overwhelmingly a pop show. Like headmasters showing their faces at the senior prom early in the evening their presence is tolerated but it's expected that they will withdraw before the misbehaviour gets going.

On this particular occasion Sir Georg left well before it got going. He left because the show began with the KLF and a group called Extreme Noise Terror.

They were loud. Let me rephrase that. They were insanely loud.

They were so loud that even a theatre full of loud music professionals, people who had spent hours of their lives being exposed
to studio playbacks through giant speakers situated in hazardous
proximity and would therefore be in the judgement of some med-
ical professionals clinically deaf, even they turned to each other
and mouthed the words, 'God alive, that's loud.'

They were so loud that the first thing I registered was the aforementioned Sir Georg Solti dashing up the aisle in the direction of
the foyer clutching his ears. On his face was a look of fear and
incomprehension. I wasn't surprised. The band were so loud that
night that I think he would have had to get as far as High Street
Kensington before he could safely remove his hands from his ears.

In the world of rock they sometimes say, not entirely jokingly,
if it's too loud you're too old. I think what they mean is if you can't
surrender to the sensory overload which is all part of the rock
experience then you will never understand the real meaning of
the rock experience. And I'm here to tell you they have a point.

If there's one thing that separates the world of rock and pop
from the musical traditions that preceded it it's the question of
amplification and what it's there to achieve. When Bill Haley's
'Rock Around The Clock' was first released in Britain in 1954 it
wasn't particularly successful. It was only when teenagers heard it
for the first time in a cinema the following year on the soundtrack
of *Blackboard Jungle*, and heard it at standard cinema volume,
that it seemed exciting. It was only when it was loud that they
responded to it and started dancing in the aisles.

But volume was never there simply to carry the signal further.
It was there to change the nature of the signal itself. The Bob
Dylan who arrived in New York in 1961 was an acoustic artist. It

was him, his harmonica and an acoustic guitar. Therefore people were comfortable calling him a folk artist and imputing to him all the perceived authenticity that went along with that descriptor.

When Bob Dylan played the Newport Folk Festival in 1965 he took the stage for the second show with the Paul Butterfield Blues Band and played an electric set. The fathers of the folk revival, people like Pete Seeger, who liked to feel they were the arbiters of acceptability, were outraged. Seeger in fact went to the sound desk and remonstrated with the engineers to turn it down. They refused, saying this was how Bob wanted it to sound.

Seeger's argument was that it was so loud and distorted you could no longer hear the song. He had nothing against amplification per se – in fact bluesman Howlin' Wolf had performed an electric show the day before and he'd had no problem with that – but he held the old-fashioned view that you amplified music in order to make it more audible. What Bob Dylan was doing was something very different. He was amplifying music in order to utterly transform it.

Dylan was less bothered about people catching the wordplay in the third verse of 'Maggie's Farm', the number he began with, than he was about exposing people to the visceral attack of his new sound. He wanted to bombard their senses. It wasn't until the end of the number that he could hear that some of the audience at least didn't approve and felt they ought to make their disapproval plain by booing.

He got the same reaction the following year when he played England with the Band. Some people felt that his music was no longer real music now that it was played on electric instruments. It was a betrayal. At Manchester Free Trade Hall somebody chose their moment in the silence between numbers to shout 'Judas!' Never again would anybody heckle a rock star with a quote from the Bible. Dylan turned to the Band and said – I shall spare you the intervening expletive – 'Play loud.'

That is still one of the less worthy reasons bands play loud. They do it simply to subdue the audience. When a rock band is in full effect there is very little an audience can do to show their appreciation or disapprobation. The band have got the artillery and therefore they hold all the cards. I refer to it as weaponry advisedly. One of the first groups to deliberately use volume as a tool were the Who back in 1966. Their record 'My Generation' used the feedback, the accidental interference caused by having a guitar and an amplifier in close proximity and turning them up loud, as part of the music.

Around about this time they went to an equipment manufacturer called Jim Marshall and told him they wanted him to provide them with 'bigger weapons'. He went away and built his famous Marshall Stacks. These were walls of amplifiers stacked on top of each other in a manner designed to enthral and intimidate their (mainly male) fans. Stacking them up placed the amplifier level with the guitarist's pick-up in order to encourage feedback. I can remember going to gigs in the early seventies and spending hours looking at the equipment arrayed on stage, like cavalry officers inspecting the cannon that were about to consume us. It's only years later that I learned that many of the cabinets were empty. That didn't matter. The visual impression of all that volume was sufficient itself.

Around about the same time, Jimi Hendrix was using the force field created by the guitar and amplifier to conjure all sorts of noises nobody had ever heard before. That had always been one of the key appeals about the electric guitar: you could make it sound like anything but a guitar – and volume was a huge part of that. Hendrix's music could not have been played quietly. It was a product of sheer volume as well as artistry. A large part of the artistry of the guitar heroes was how they managed the volume.

Sheer volume is one key feature of modern pop music. You can't escape it. The other feature is the repetition. If you think pop music has become more relentless in recent years you wouldn't be wrong. There's a reason for that.

Dance records used to be able to maintain the beat until the drummer succumbed to exhaustion. This changed in the late seventies when drum machines started to take over. Drum machines don't succumb to exhaustion and, as the old joke goes, you only have to punch in the instructions once, which makes them easier to deal with than the average drummer. The mechanization of rhythm has fundamentally changed the nature of music-making in the modern age.

Most records on the charts nowadays have been built in a way that wouldn't have made any sense to the hit makers of the sixties. As John Seabrook describes it in his excellent book *The Song Machine*, they are now built on a chassis of percussion. All the component parts are contracted out to specialists. The track people invent the grooves. The hook people write the catchy bits. The top line people come up with the bit the singer sings.

A modern hit record is precisely assembled over a long period for maximum commercial appeal. Because much of the process of assembly takes place on machines and the building can be witnessed on screens, all the stakeholders get involved and there's a general compulsion to make sure that every last inch of the spectrum is filled. Hence the most common complaint about contemporary popular music, even from the people who like it, is that it lacks dynamic range. Record companies used to pay a lot of money to the people who produced the records. They now pay it to the people who master the records, whose special skill is to load the signal with as much noise as possible.

As in every other area, technology has levelled the playing field, putting basic competence within the reach of more people. Before multitrack recording and digital rhythm tracks, making music was like using a manual typewriter. Your first decision had best be the right one because it couldn't easily be undone. Nowadays everything is provisional. Most dance records – and most contemporary pop records are dance records – are never exactly finished. They're always up for further changes. In 1982 the producer Arthur Baker was asked what he did for a living. 'I remix a record called "Walking On Sunshine",' he said. At the time it seemed like a joke. Now it seems realistic.

The other thing that's disappeared in this appliance of science is the idea of development within a record. Events no longer unfold. The record is largely the same at the end as it was in the beginning. This is logical. Because if you've got a committee making a record – and all pop singles are made by committee nowadays – they're going to insist that you put the most commercially appealing elements of the record in the shop window. Story songs are rare these days. As soon as listeners have found a bit of a record that they like they prefer to stay in that moment for ten minutes rather than go anywhere else.

The audience for contemporary pop records has never known a

world where they couldn't call up a reliably pleasurable experience with one click of their thumb. They have grown up in a world where you can buy bags of your favourite sweet, thereby escaping the Russian roulette of the assortment. They have never known a world where you couldn't watch your favourite TV programme until you were sick of it. No surprise that their big hit records are made up exclusively of the catchy bits.

That's why drugs have been so closely associated with the clubbing experience. The aim is to block out everything else and just take moments of pleasure and prolong them endlessly. Of course as you get older you realize that you can't prolong moments of pleasure. That's why they're pleasure. If they're prolonged they become tedious. You realize that in order for there to be loud there first has to be quiet.

Pete Townshend, who was one of the first to call for bigger weapons, was the first to complain that he was going deaf as a consequence. Every grown-up in rock and roll knows that this is a serious issue. However, rather than do the obvious thing, which would be to turn it down, they attempt to mitigate the effects with ear defenders. I know at least one club DJ who makes sure he wears earplugs in order to protect himself from the sound he himself is making.

It's a good job Sir Georg Solti didn't try clubbing. The music in clubs is played at an even more threatening volume and it is part of the clubbing experience that it should be played relentlessly. In a club you feel the sound waves advancing upon you until they threaten to collapse your ribcage. Is this pleasure? Yes, of a sort, but it's like smoking and drinking in that you have to be trained to it. Nobody in their right mind would take to it on their own.

I have a theory about musical genres. It is one of the few things that applies equally across the musical spectrum. It's this. The quality the detractors see as a shortcoming is the very thing the disciples like. The average teenager doesn't like classical music because it takes too long to get going, doesn't like jazz because it wanders away from the melody, and doesn't like country music because it's too sentimental. Those are the same qualities that the people who like those forms of music like about them. The same thing applies from the opposite side of the gulf of incomprehension. What rock's detractors don't like about it is its volume. What dance music's detractors don't like is its repetition. It's no more use to expect pop music to be less noisy and less repetitious than it is to expect classical music to get to its point more directly. In both cases it is what it is.

WHAT USE ARE DJS?

In the 1973 George Lucas film *American Graffiti* the young
hero, played by Richard Dreyfuss, wishes to make contact
with the attractive blonde who's been making eyes at him
as he drives around his small California town on a hot summer's evening. So he does what anyone would have done in the
days before social media. He turns up at the local radio station in
person late at night to see if he can somehow get a message put out
on the airwaves, preferably by the DJ whose voice he hears over
those airwaves, the man whose charismatic growl has earned him
fame as Wolfman Jack. The Wolfman, he reasons, is in a uniquely
privileged position and may be the only person who can make his
dream come true.

When he gets to the radio station he meets the one individual
on the premises at that time of night. This man explains that he's

not Wolfman Jack. He's just the man who plays in the voice of Wolfman Jack from tapes. Richard leaves disillusioned, the romantic idea of the special status of the radio DJ – an idea he has constructed in his head over many years – shattered.

That was how it was depicted in the film, which was set in 1962 and made over ten years later. The golden days of the radio DJ were apparently gone.

Pop fans always like to feel there was a time in the past when things were real, and the figure of the lone DJ actually sitting over a turntable and playing the records that spoke from his heart is one of those ideas that refuses to die. It lived on in the 1971 thriller *Play Misty for Me*, where Clint Eastwood was threatened with death when he didn't play a listener request, and in more than one elegiac song that mourned the passing of the lone DJ who barricaded himself into his booth rather than give in to the management who wanted to change the format of the station or otherwise interfere with the integrity of his calling.

BBC's Broadcasting House now has a Peel Wing, named after the Radio 1 DJ who died in 2004. There are Peel lectures in his memory. The fiftieth anniversary of Radio 1 in 2017 was marked with many celebrations of his unique role in the station's history, even though he was always at pains to put clear water between himself and the station's objectives and in the years I had anything to do with him always conducted himself like a man who felt he was about to be fired any day. He would have thought the idea of his ending up a national treasure absolutely hilarious.

But the idea of the renegade DJ is one that lives in our imagined past. When I was growing up in the sixties the veterans of the First World War were still among us and the veterans of the Second were our parents and therefore entirely unremarkable. It was only when the passage of time meant that survivors were no longer with us that everybody started to get so exercised about the business of remembrance. It's only when something has slipped away that we venerate it.

Something similar is happening with the DJ. It's curious how the idea of the passionate independent DJ is exalted and celebrated while everywhere you look, both in the private and public sectors, the people who run the radio stations are doing everything in their power to drive the renegade DJ to extinction. Sometimes those people deny doing any such thing. Sometimes they don't. A few years ago I asked the head of programming at one major commercial broadcaster, 'Is there anyone still on the radio who chooses their own records?' He raised a satirical eyebrow and said, 'I very much hope not.'

Even though that's the last impression they ever wish to give, radio stations are in my experience the most tightly controlled of all media operations. There are more and more radio outlets and less and less autonomy granted to the people who run them. There was a time, at the end of the last century, where the thinking was that technology and the internet would bring about a broadcasting renaissance, enabling a thousand flowers to bloom, facilitating the growth of an untold number of stations offering all manner of different varieties of music and different sorts of presentation. This, you may have noticed, hasn't happened. Instead of a thousand flowers blooming the same technology has enabled a few very powerful gardeners to dictate exactly which blooms should flourish and when and where. This drive for control has been facilitated by the very technology that everyone thought would set us free.

Most music radio is now a branch of the information technology industry. It is run by algorithms.

How can you tell? Well, a lot of trouble is gone to to ensure you *can't* tell. Most music radio you hear nowadays isn't coming from records. It's being played in from a hard drive. All the music on the hard drive has been chosen by the management with the aid of powerful algorithms that tell them what has proved popular in the past. The role of the individual DJ in choosing anything but a tiny percentage of the output – a role which was always overstated, usually by the DJs – is now negligible.

The traditional role of radio, which was to provide company, has been in some cases further betrayed by the fact that the live-sounding exchange you're hearing was actually recorded ten minutes earlier and has then been tidied up in the edit. While you're listening to that one they're busy recording another. The fact that somebody can go to such trouble to make something sound live boggles the mind. Wouldn't it be easier just to do it live in the first place? But that would mean sacrificing control, and that they will never do. Visiting most radio stations today I am reminded of what they used to say about Los Angeles. There is no there there.

Meanwhile in the world of electronic dance music the DJ is more important than ever. According to the business magazine *Forbes* the top ten dance music DJs earned over $274 million in 2014. The best of them can be paid a quarter of a million dollars for playing records from a laptop. Those records will be a combination of records made by others and their own personal mixes which maximize whatever happens to be their signature sound. These people aren't just paid on reputation. They're paid because they get results. Particularly in the high-end clubs of Las Vegas, where electronic dance music competes for the leisure dollar with the traditional star vehicle stage show – the clubs where holiday-ing footballers and hedge fund bosses drop five figures and more for a bottle of champagne – these DJs are highly prized for their ability to judge the mood of a roomful of what the papers would call revellers and tactically deploy their favourite tactic, the drop, in which the music is suddenly replaced with the primal throb of the rhythm track and the whole room points its fingers in the air as if in the direction of some unseen god. Those are the moments for which dance DJs command sums of money that even musi-cians cannot match. These days the biggest DJs only go on the radio when they feel in need of a little flattery. Their real work is out there where the people are.

It's a striking contrast. The radio DJ is now essentially the customer-facing element of the large conglomerate. He's there to make them look as if they're not a large conglomerate. His most important attribute is his ability to project some sort of personal-ity. To do what radio DJs have done through the years, which is essentially talk while thinking about something else altogether. The club DJ, on the other hand, doesn't have to speak. He just has to do. He's the high priest who can join heaven and earth. It's odd that radio should be downgrading one sort at the same time as the world of clubbing is putting the other sort on a pedestal such as he has never mounted before.

The role of the DJ in picking the actual records has never been clear. The picture of the pirate DJ playing his favourites on some bucking freighter in the North Sea was something more honoured in the breach than the observance. The whole idea of what a DJ was expected to do was challenged in court in 1994 when the former Radio 1 DJ Bruno Brookes came up against the former Radio 1 DJ Bob Harris over the question of whether Bob's records were the tools of his trade or just a nice asset to have. Bob argued successfully that in his case they were the tools of his trade. Many other DJs didn't really know what he was talking about.

But does this matter to anyone except old DJs and old romantics like me? The radio DJ seems to me to be going the way of the blacksmith, harried to extinction by a number of different forces. Greater audience choice means the biggest names of today are not as household-name familiar as the big names of the seventies were in their supermarket-opening prime. Radio stations hire people who are known from the TV to present their programmes because in this world name recognition has a greater value than skill. Music streaming now means that the listeners have access to just as much music as the people in the radio stations, calling into question why anybody should ring up and ask to hear anything in particular when they can presumably play it themselves. Radio stations now have far stricter rules on what they will play and what they will not play and what the presenters, who are inappropriately referred to as 'the talent', are allowed to say in between them.

I don't get the feeling that there has been a great new DJ in years, which may account for the fact that the old ones seem to hang around far longer than anyone would have predicted back in the 1970s. Furthermore, radio DJs are also victims of the fact that we live in a more censorious age than ever before, thanks to social media, and the words and actions that people used to ascribe to personal eccentricities, such as when Mike Read suddenly decided to be offended by Frankie Goes to Hollywood in 1984 and took off their record halfway through, are now the kind of things that would earn you a few weeks in the digital stocks and would result in some form of public apology. Because their job was essentially to sit in a soundproof room talking to themselves it's no surprise that so many DJs seemed to have only a tenuous grip on reality. Nowadays they're all too sane. In fact they probably call themselves music presenters rather than DJs. In that sense radio DJs have lost an empire and not yet found a role.

The great thing about the club DJ, on the other hand, is that he presides over a genuine shared experience. He reads the room. He judges the crowd's mood and reaches into his box and picks the precise record that he believes will raise their mood a few notches higher. He feels the moment just as the crowd does because he's living through that moment with them. He's not operating according to a plan arrived at a week earlier or a day earlier. There is no algorithm, no playlist software, no committee of wise heads that can ever replace that particular magic. And as the record plays he's in the room, enjoying it every bit as much as the audience. He isn't talking to a producer or popping outside for a smoke. He is fulfilling his side of the ancient compact, in which he has produced a record, held it up, looked you in the eye and said, 'I think you're going to like this,' and then stuck around to see if you do. He is living in the moment, ideally the same ecstatic moment as the audience. That's as real as pop gets.

ANGELS AT FUNERALS

Last year I was asked for the first time to provide the music for the funeral of a former colleague. I wasn't required to play the music, I was asked to provide the recorded music. And the music wasn't to be played in church. It was intended to accompany a gathering of a couple of hundred family, friends and former colleagues taking place after the service in a moderately smart setting.

Now that it's clear it's not going to go away, pop music is increasingly called upon to fulfil its responsibilities by soundtracking our great rites of passage. I was asked to provide this service because I supposedly know a lot about popular music. That always worries me. If you do know a lot about music the two things you know best are, one, there's lots of music you don't know, and two, it's all a question of taste and how emotionally receptive you happen to be at the moment it falls upon your ear.

I sat down to prepare a playlist. At my fingertips I had just about everything ever recorded. Not that I own everything ever recorded but in this day and age the internet means we all have access to more music than even the BBC would have had access to thirty years ago.

The difficulty with pop music and funerals is that when you start choosing tracks to go on your compilation tape, or in my case a Spotify playlist, you very quickly realize that so much pop music seems to fall into one of two camps. Either it's 'Gloomy Sunday' or it's 'Zip-A-Dee Doo-Dah'. Neither is acceptable. You can't pick a piece of self-consciously depressing music for a funeral playlist – like, say, Joy Division's 'Love Will Tear Us Apart' or Johnny Cash's 'Hurt' – because it will seem as though you're tastelessly trying to tip people into tears. On the other hand you can't play happy music like Abba because, well, you just can't.

If you choose a piece of music that seems to be trying to match the occasion, say Bob Dylan's 'Knockin' On Heaven's Door', you will quite rightly be accused of indulging yourself. If on the other hand you choose something simply because you happen to like it, like the Beatles' 'Penny Lane' for instance, you will be accused of rampant insensitivity.

The first problem is that most pop music has words. People have a tendency to overlook lyrics if they're confident that the sound of the song hits what they think is the right note. That's why Percy Sledge's 'When A Man Loves A Woman' remains unaccountably popular at weddings, despite it being a song about the dangers of marrying an unfaithful woman. Most of the words of popular songs work upon us because they have the magical power of being able to whisk us away from our present surroundings to some sort of happy place. This is inappropriate at a funeral.

The overpowering fear of anyone putting together a list of pop songs to be played at a wake is that conversation will be stilted and there will be inevitable silences during which a few lines from one of your less fortunate choices will seem to be the loudest sound on earth and will have the entire room thinking, 'What was he thinking of when he chose this?'

However, I set to work. Using all my experience I put together a playlist that, with a bit of luck, would be easy to ignore if you wanted to ignore it and similarly easy to warm to if that was your inclination. The secret of a playlist – any playlist – is that its core should not be too predictable and its surprises should be minor and delightful rather than sudden and jarring. It should be able to satisfy people who really don't listen to much music at all as a rule and also to elicit the grudging appreciation of the tiny number of advanced musical snobs who are bound to be represented in any gathering of a few hundred people.

What sort of things? Well, I started off with instrumental music, which at least ensured that the party coming back from the crematorium wouldn't walk into the room to be greeted by anything too insensitive to their mood. Here there are rules that can be helpful. I chose Duke Ellington because old jazz always sounds joyous but somehow poignant. Then I mixed in wide swathes of what we now call world music, which is difficult to take exception to because we don't understand the words. Then I added some music from films that nobody can quite remember the name of. And then later on I mixed in the crowd at his favourite football ground and lots of Irish music because everybody seems to agree to be Irish on these occasions. I think I may have identified the sweet spot of this kind of approach. It's 'Danny Boy' as played by the saxophonist Ben Webster. By then I hoped the mood in the room would be sentimental but stable – stable enough to be able to tolerate Ella Fitzgerald doing 'Manhattan' and Crowded House's 'Weather With You'. Anybody who was still there three hours later for Elvis Costello doing 'She' and Al Green singing 'Take Me To The River' would have presumably taken enough drink to no longer be in the mood to turn up their noses at any of the choices. It seemed to work.

Much as the churches of the nation are slowly being converted into fitness studios and night clubs, so pop music is edging out sacred music in the great ceremonies of hatch, match and despatch. 'Nimrod' is being supplanted by Robbie Williams' 'Angels', 'Abide With Me' by Monty Python's 'Always Look On The Bright Side Of Life'. Although I note that the Co-operative Funeral Service will have no truck with 'Imagine', not on the grounds that it's a ropey song but because it promotes the idea of a world with no heaven as being somehow desirable.

You would expect me to approve of this, the apparent final triumph of pop music, but I'm not sure I do. For a variety of reasons. For one, turning one's funeral into the *Desert Island Discs* you were never invited to take part in during your life doesn't seem like a good idea. People traditionally use music as a way to position themselves and it seems particularly redundant and tasteless to do this after you've gone. The notion that your nearest and dearest should think any more or less about you because you always had good taste in B-sides seems like taking neediness to new lengths.

The more people know about the music the more likely they are to do this. As your favourite music plays there will be at least one of your old friends in the church reflecting on the fact that they escaped all those times you tried to get them to listen to this – no, *really* listen to this – when you were alive and now here they are, stuck in church, wondering when it's going to end. In these circumstances they will not be thinking kindly of you.

We now live in the world of customized vows, where the off-the-peg solution no longer seems equal to people's needs, where the standard musical selection is too confining of everybody's presumed giant personality. I went to the funerals of all my parents' generation and 'Abide With Me' was about as indulgent as it got. Just as a wedding is now increasingly all about personal fulfilment rather than a commitment to continuity and is marked by songs like 'I Will Always Love You', which is less a vow than a boast, so people who've lived lives of blameless anonymity are now delivered into the hereafter to the strains of Frank Sinatra's ridiculous 'My Way', a song which is the very definition of building up your part in life. When it comes to finding music for funerals, pop music always seems to be straining for a weight which doesn't come naturally to it.

It doesn't really have an agreed repertoire it can reach for at times like this. I've always liked the idea of those funerals in the Deep South where people, regardless of what godless lives they've led, revert to tradition, as people generally do at times of great stress, and sing 'Will The Circle Be Unbroken?' I like the idea that you choose music to express your kinship with the rest of humanity rather than your difference from it.

I have always been attracted by the idea of a memorial service which is as standard as they come, where the liturgy is the kind of thing that people can mumble without thinking, where the hymns are the kind that you can sing without needing to consult the hymn book, where the thrust of the whole service is that the deceased has gone off to join the choir invisible in what Alan Bennett called 'the magnificent equality of death'. It finishes with one of Strauss's last songs. As the congregation make their way out of the church into the sunlight and traffic, that sound fades and is mixed into the bright, brassy, heedlessly pleasure-seeking sound of, say, Martha and the Vandellas' 'Dancing In The Street'.

That's where pop music belongs. Pop music is to do with life and the enjoyment thereof. It doesn't have a lot to say about mortality. In fact, the greatest pop songs celebrate the beginnings of experiences, not their endings. They are about walking into the room at the party. They're about catching somebody's eye across a crowded dance floor. When it tries to gather itself to do death it always sounds as though pop's getting ideas above its station. It has no business with a ceremony like this because pop is essentially about getting things out of proportion, whereas a funeral is about the opposite. Pop is dedicated to the proposition that this moment is like no other, this girl is like no other, and nobody ever suffered a hurt such as the songwriter is enduring at the moment of writing this song.

George Harrison died in 2001. Along with Paul McCartney, John Lennon and Ringo Starr, he was, it seems plain, responsible for the generation of more joy than most of us. And what was their reward? Lennon was murdered by a fan. George was attacked in his own home in the middle of the night by a deranged obsessive, an attack that contributed towards his early death. Interestingly,

George was always interested in death. He had written more songs about death than any of his peers. He'd been thinking about it from the time he became interested in Eastern religion in the late sixties. At the age of twenty-five he was writing songs like 'The Art Of Dying' and 'All Things Must Pass'. A year after his death his friends and fans gathered at the Albert Hall to mark his life. They played all his great songs, many of which were straining towards a spiritual dimension, and they played them well.

Right at the very end a man in his early seventies with a distinctive bog brush haircut came to the front of the stage with his ukulele. Joe Brown was a star before the Beatles were heard of outside Liverpool and, like George, he was an enthusiastic user of that least portentous, least self-important of instruments. You can play anything on a ukulele and it will always sound modest and charming and oddly moving. The song he played that night, 'I'll See You In My Dreams', was written in the 1920s and had on the face of it nothing to do with George Harrison. In this case it worked because he sang it beautifully and he had the personality to carry it off. It worked because it wasn't trying to be equal to the occasion. It worked, as pop music so often does, because it caught its audience unawares. It worked because it was a light thing presented in a context which was anything but light. It worked because it fulfilled the real sacred duty of all pop music, which is not to give us a life-changing experience, nor a brand-new perspective on life and mortality, nothing big and heavy like that, but to provide that one quality that has kept me coming back for fifty years. A lift.

4
TAP DANCING ABOUT ARCHITECTURE

THE QUESTION I DREAD
THE MOST

A t a drinks do the other day a woman asked me the question I dread the most: 'What kind of music do you like?' I know she was only trying to make small talk. I really shouldn't shrivel up the way I do. I wouldn't have had a problem if she'd said, 'Read any good books lately?' or 'Have you been on holiday yet?' because those questions demand direct, specific answers.

Two kinds of people ask me the 'what kind of music?' question. There are those who don't know I've got the better part of twenty thousand records at home and therefore my relationship with music could be said to be complicated.

Then there are the people who know I've got a lot of records and expect me to be somehow expert in predicting what they might like.

In truth there is nothing you can say in response to this

question that doesn't make you sound like either a dunderhead or a raging pseud.

I've heard all these and more. I've probably said some of them. 'Anything with a good tune' is the only honest answer but it's been unusable since 1965. 'You probably wouldn't have heard of them' makes you sound seventeen years old, which is the emotional age of most men when it comes to discussing music. 'Coldplay and Beyoncé' makes you sound like a sheep. 'The Arctic Monkeys' makes you sound like Gordon Brown. 'Anything but country and western' marks you out as both snob and moron. 'I don't like music' is just plain rude. 'Oh, bit of trance, bit of rare groove et cetera' makes you sound like a cloth-eared category shopper. 'Oh, I always think Louis Armstrong had a point when he said there were just two kinds of music: good and bad' makes you sound pompous enough to punch.

To avoid any of these and other catastrophes I tend to look down and mumble, 'All sorts of things,' at which point my interlocutor will invariably say, 'Oh, like me!'

That's the interesting thing about taste. Everyone thinks theirs is broad. Mostly it's not. When you've worked around music and music fiends as long as I have you learn that only a tiny handful of people are familiar with a wide range of music and have catholic taste when it comes to appreciating it. And they tend to keep quiet about it because they know how much they don't know.

Anyway, at the drinks do my wife appeared and rescued me mid-mumble with a change of subject. I've thought about it a lot since. I think in future if people ask me what kind of music I like I shall respond brightly with 'The Beatles!'

At least it's honest.

EVERYTHING I KNOW
ABOUT THE BLUES

In 1978 I spent a few days in Memphis, Tennessee in the company of Alex Chilton. A former member of local groups Big Star and the Box Tops, Chilton was a passionate advocate of the unique contribution made by his city and its outlying regions to popular music. One morning I was woken by a call from him. 'I'm downstairs in the lobby,' he said. 'I want to show you where the blues came from.'

He was waiting outside, barefoot and leaning against a battered Volkswagen. He hadn't been to bed. The previous evening we had been at a reception thrown by the city fathers in an antebellum white mansion. R&B veteran Rufus Thomas had been the greeter and liveried servants had dispensed mint juleps to local worthies and visiting media as the powers behind the Memphis Blues Festival toasted their city's heritage.

Chilton proposed a trip as an antidote to the previous evening. He aimed his car through the city's southern suburbs. After half an hour the housing petered out and we found ourselves on a flat, straight road built on a causeway slightly raised above brown agricultural land on either side. We crossed the state line into Mississippi in the direction of Clarksdale on Highway 61, where even the meanest road signs have a magic resonance. Highway 61 takes you in the direction of Tunica, Indianola, Vicksburg, Rolling Fork, Fayette, Rosedale, Belzoni, Natchez, China Grove and Clarksdale on the road which accompanies the Mississippi down to the Gulf of Mexico.

Rosedale is where Robert Johnson was going with his rider by his side in his signature song 'Crossroads'. Indianola is where B. B. King was born and worked as a tractor driver for a dollar a day. Little Brother Montgomery played the 'Vicksburg Blues'. Rolling Fork was the birthplace of Muddy Waters. Son House came from Clarksdale.

There is no comparable patch of the earth's surface. Nowhere else can boast an influential body of music to compare with this tiny pocket of land. As the alluvial plain slipped by each place name triggered a tune in my memory.

The Mississippi Delta is good farming land but charmless territory, slightly spooky even in broad daylight. At one junction Chilton took a right into a small town and we cruised slowly past neat, white timber-frame houses where retired country people were fixing cars or mowing lawns. Then the VW bumped over an unguarded level crossing to the other side of the tracks. Here every face was black and looked back with suspicion. Chilton pulled over at a small general store that sold household goods such as ironing boards, cleaning materials and small electrical appliances.

Near the back was a small section in which you could buy charms and good-luck potions, small tinted bottles of mysterious liquids, sold inside cotton bags held closed with a drawstring. 'Mojo hands,' Chilton explained. The lady behind the counter, clearly unused to white customers, gave us a neutral stare. We bought some books of spells and returned to the car.

Chilton turned the car off the main street on to an unmade road and we headed away from town and into the woods. The timber-frame houses gave way to older, less well-maintained properties which steadily shrank in size and prestige until they were tiny shacks that seemed to have been assembled without conventional building materials. Ancient cars, long ago cannibalized for their last spare part, lay crippled on front yards. Undernourished dogs sniffed the unmade road. Occasionally a pair of children's eyes would peer out from within. Whatever kind of poverty this was, it appeared to exist beyond the reach of social services.

Chilton nosed the car further on until we came to the levee (the raised earthworks designed to prevent the catastrophic consequences of a repeat of the floods of the twenties) and beyond it the brown, broad, sluggish Mississippi, the most hymned river on earth.

One of the aspects of the blues most appealing to the European ear is the words of the songs, particularly the names of towns, highways, people or geographical features. To the people who came up with, wrote, adapted or borrowed these names, they were markers on a mental map of a land as familiar to them as the Tube might be to a Londoner. But to a British teenager tuning in to

Sonny Boy Williamson or Elmore James in the late sixties they read like metaphors of dread, like places on a map of Middle Earth. Actually visiting them was deeply strange.

Back in 1978 there would probably have been old people in that area who might have actually heard Delta musicians such as Robert Johnson and Son House in their prime, before the area was depopulated by progress, the extension of civil rights, the lure of the cities and the mechanization of the cotton industry. Much had changed but what remained was the desolation of the place, even one hundred years after the alleged emancipation of the slaves.

Every blues singer and scholar has a pat answer to the question 'What is the blues?' Is it African music in America? Is it a woman; a feeling; a three-line AAB verse form; three chords – the first, the fourth and the fifth; 'the spiritual energy of the church thrust into the eyes of life's raw realities', as one scholar said; a low-down shaking chill; the conception of aching hearts; a defiance of the undertaker; the acceptance of anguish leading to joy? Or is it the humdrum feeling that you've been caught in a rain of soup and you ain't got nothin' but a fork?

Whatever the blues is, you could imagine it being born in precisely this kind of place. One of the most common lines in the blues – and this is a music full of common lines – goes 'you can't lose what you never had'. In this bleak land most people had nothing. Here people had to do back-breaking work all day to get their hands on the slightest something, knowing that something might then be taken away at any time by economic circumstances, the Jim Crow laws, the weather, the boll weevil, the flood, their neighbour, the police, the overseers, even the lynch mob.

Had Chilton been right when he said this was where the blues came from? Certainly this strangely joyous music of consolation emerged out of Mississippi at the turn of the century. Some disciples of Charley Patton are even prepared to locate its birthplace more specifically to the Dockery plantation in Sunflower County. Patton's is one of the first names to be attached to recordings. He was born in 1891 and died in 1934. He was straight-haired, a mix of black, white and native American.

Patton sounds like precisely nobody else. He sings hard, growling right from the back of the throat and punishing his guitar in patterns that have since found their way into literally tens of thousands of records. When Patton was singing 'High Water Everywhere' in 1929 Bing Crosby was crooning 'Ol' Man River' with Paul Whiteman. They were singing about the same river but they could have been on different planets.

The American Congress declared 2003 the Year of the Blues, kicking off twelve months of Volkswagen-sponsored activities meant to highlight the contribution made by this music to the culture of America and the world. Then there was a seven-film series called *Martin Scorsese Presents the Blues*. Scorsese directed the first episode, 'Feel Like Going Home', which attempts to trace the kinship between the music of the Delta and the music of Mali.

The argument for the linkage between African music and the blues seems less persuasive than the historical fact that during the slave time the Africans were denied access to any musical instruments (particularly the drums). Therefore when they got a degree of emancipation, music was the cheapest and most powerful means of expressing their humanity – of saying, 'We are here.'

The 2003 centenary marks the hundred years since the night when W. C. Handy, a professional musician and band leader, was reputedly waiting at a railway station in Tutwiler, Mississippi. He found himself sharing a bench with an old black man in rags who was playing an ancient guitar and sliding a knife up and down the neck to echo the words of his song. This was one line repeated three times about 'going where the Southern crosses the dog' (a reference to the nearby intersection of two railroads, suggesting this man had made up the song himself). The combination of the ghostly sound of the guitar and the opaqueness of the lyric made Handy years later describe it as 'the weirdest music I had ever heard'.

Handy was an experienced American musician who came from the South and had travelled all over the American continent, yet he had never heard this music which had presumably been under his nose. There was no radio at the time. Only things written down on sheet music survived. Handy had heard field hollers and work songs and spirituals and he knew that there were black folk musicians who accompanied themselves on cheap guitars from mail order catalogues, but he had to ask the man what kind of music he was playing. The man had no answer. Handy went down in history as the Father of the Blues largely because he was the first man to give it a name.

The day following my trip down the Delta with Chilton I went to W. C. Handy Park in Memphis to attend the Blues Festival. Handy Park is just off Beale Street, the black man's Broadway of yore, which at the time was in the process of being demolished in the name of urban renewal. Elvis had died the year before and Memphis was temporarily confused, yet to realize its future as a heritage site and tourist destination. One of the acts on stage that day was local musician Furry Lewis.

Furry's career followed a classic blues trajectory. He started off as a street musician after the First World War, travelling occasionally by hopping freights. An accident on one such journey resulted in his losing a leg. By the end of the twenties he had attracted sufficient attention in Memphis to be asked to go north to Chicago to record for the Vocalion label. A few thousand copies of his recordings may have been pressed but they didn't sell particularly well. Two years later the Depression meant that the companies abruptly stopped making records for the blues market and the demand for live music dried up. This explains why the overwhelming majority of classic country blues recordings were made in a tiny window between 1928 and 1930.

Furry put away his guitar, getting a job working for the Memphis sanitation department. By the end of World War Two the old country blues sounded tame next to the urban variety of music being made in the cities by Mississippi émigrés like Muddy Waters. Furry's music was an anachronism.

In 1959, twenty-five years after Lewis had stopped regarding himself as a professional musician, he was tracked down by Sam Charters, a white producer, historian and blues fan who treasured Lewis's early 78s. (How much these 78s must have been cherished we can only imagine. If one broke there was no way of replacing it.) Charters bought him a guitar and persuaded him that the groundswell of interest in folk music among the student community meant it was worth him going into the studio to record again. Thus for the last twenty years of his life Lewis enjoyed the curious sensation of being courted by the white society whose streets he had been sweeping all these years. Before his death in 1981 he opened for Leon Russell, appeared in a film with Burt Reynolds and was profiled in *Playboy*.

You could apply his story, with variations, to the lives of other country bluesmen: to Bukka White, who did time in Mississippi's notorious Parchman Farm in the thirties for shooting a man and was later 'found' by scholar and guitarist John Fahey after he posted a letter to 'Booker T. Washington White (Old Blues Singer) c/o General Delivery, Aberdeen, Mississippi'.

You could say something similar about Mississippi John Hurt, who had only ever travelled away from the tiny town of Avalon to make a record in Memphis in the late 1920s, who gave up music during the Depression and was working for $28 a month as a farmhand. Hurt assumed the only reason a white man would come knocking on his door was because he had done something wrong.

You could say it about Son House, the man who taught Robert Johnson, who was found in New York State in 1964 and visited London in 1970.

These are unimaginable life experiences. Most of these men were born into poverty, knew little education, and took up the guitar because they had the vague feeling that they had some talent and would do anything to escape the onerous physical labour that would otherwise be their lot. Their decision to play the blues meant instant estrangement from the God-fearing members of their families. They played in the streets, on the porch of the general store, at turpentine camps or house parties until they were invited to do the same thing for money and whisky at juke joints.

It's difficult to credit now, listening to these trebly recordings through the surface noise of the ancient 78s they have been remastered from, but these people played for dancing. Cars were almost unknown out in the country. There was little background noise for the musicians to compete against, only the sound of the crowd or the occasional fight. They hammered away and slammed their feet down on the floor to drive the dancers. Listen to Charley Patton or Son House and you hear the guitar used essentially as a percussion instrument.

On Saturday afternoons and evenings the only thing to do was go into town, get drunk on moonshine whisky, play cards, dance and fight. Violence was a fact of life. They learned to keep going through shootings and stabbings. The police accepted a certain level of violent death among blacks as the cost of doing business. The Clarksdale newspaper had a column set aside for court reporting of cases involving black people. It was called 'Good Mawnin Judge'.

If they became popular enough they might make their way either on foot or via a slow-moving train to Henry C. Speir's music store in Jackson, Mississippi. If they impressed Mr Speir he might arrange for them to go to one of the cities to record for a company such as Paramount or Gennett or Vocalion. This might take place in a hotel room or in an office attached to a pressing plant. They would probably be given whisky to loosen them up. In one day they might record all the tunes they knew, though the men from the record companies were only interested in blues. Robert Johnson apparently liked Bing Crosby tunes but the companies knew what they could sell and what they couldn't. The musicians might return south with a hundred dollars. The important thing was to have a record which would go on the jukeboxes. That way their stock would rise and they would be able to draw more people.

Then they would get back to wandering in their haphazard way, like Robert Johnson, whose travels took him as far east as

New York and as far north as Canada. But these men never broke out of the local scene. They existed below the radar of the entertainment industry. There was nothing to be promoted towards. The odd record might find its way to one of the handful of white collectors who were developing an interest on both sides of the Atlantic but that would be wholly accidental. (Six months after Robert Johnson was killed by the poisoned whisky he had been slipped by a jealous husband, word came that John Hammond wanted him to come to New York to appear at his From Spirituals to Swing concert at Carnegie Hall, an event designed to legitimize the growing serious interest in the black folk music of America. In the event Hammond went on stage with a gramophone and played Johnson's 'Walkin' Blues' to the audience.)

For many of them the thirties meant lowering their expectations of life, letting go of whatever prominence they had achieved in their local communities and slipping back dissatisfied into the same life as the poor saps they had hoped to leave behind. They might leave the area like the hundreds of blacks who every night took the Illinois Central Railroad out of Memphis to ride the ten-hour journey to Chicago where there were jobs that paid something like a living wage. (Seventy-five thousand black people left Mississippi for Chicago in the 1940s in one of the most significant mass movements of modern times.) Maybe they might get a job on the killing floors of the Chicago stockyards. In all events they vanished into obscurity, raised families and eventually got to the point where nobody around knew they had ever been musicians, let alone well-known ones.

Then one day during the Eisenhower years a young white man with a beard might come knocking at your door asking if he was right in thinking you were a name you hadn't used for twenty years. He had a tape recorder and a bottle of whisky and asked if you still played. If you'd forgotten how, he produced a precious 78 out of his bag and offered to remind you. (Men like Son House found themselves tutored by young disciples such as Al Wilson of Canned Heat, who knew more about House's music than he did himself.)

There then followed a strange Indian summer of playing folk festivals or coffee houses in front of pretty girls with long hair and beatnik-looking guys with beards who always wanted to know about your tunings. It might mean a few dollars to buy a car, contracts with labels like Vanguard and Folkways, and sometimes even tours overseas. Mississippi John Hurt was on the TV before he owned a TV.

The country blues singers were reserved, often suspicious men, understandably convinced that this unsought good fortune might be removed as fast as it had appeared. Joni Mitchell wrote a candid song about Furry Lewis called 'Furry Sings The Blues' which captures the humming tension between the blues originals and the white establishment in whose uneasy embrace they were folded. In her song, Furry points a bony finger at his visitor and says, 'I don't like you.' Everybody laughs nervously but she recognizes that he means it and 'we're only welcome for our drink and smoke.' Elsewhere in the same song Mitchell sings about how they're tearing down old Beale Street to make parking lots.

When I returned to Memphis in the late nineties the city's legendary thoroughfare was now dedicated to getting the money from the pockets of the increasing number of tourists drawn to the city by its music connections. The demolition work that had been in full swing in 1978 had been suddenly halted, with the wrecking ball in mid-air and then flung into reverse. The facades of old buildings were held in place by scaffolding. Alongside them were the newly built B. B. King Blues Café, Elvis Presley's, the Hard Rock Café and other less obviously branded establishments where you could drink Bud and eat burgers to the accompaniment of live McBlues, music played too loud by men in shiny tour jackets and cowboy hats.

For a lot of middle-aged Americans the blues has become part of the contemporary leisure experience. In his *Martin Scorsese Presents the Blues* film 'The Road to Memphis', Richard Pearce interweaves the experiences of three men who did their time on Beale Street when it was, in the words of Rufus Thomas, 'heaven for the black man'. ('If you had one night black on Beale Street,' goes one Thomas line, 'you'd never want to be white again.') One of them is B. B. King, along with Ray Charles the last giant of the music and even at the age of seventy-eight an indefatigable touring act. He makes his way through the lobby of a Mississippi hotel on regal autopilot, accepting the proffered good wishes of middle-aged white tourists. These people may not have his records, they may not be that familiar with his piercing, needy tenor, the lowering horns that he favours or the spangled clusters of single notes that he peels like dollar bills from his guitar Lucille, but they defer to his status as King of the Blues as surely as they know the billions that McDonald's have sold.

King has been a star since the mid-1950s. He started as a DJ and the way he has managed to trim to the prevailing wind while retaining his position as blues brother number one suggests that he used the time to mark out the pitfalls others didn't see. The son of the man who drove his bus back in the sixties describes the key night in 1968 when B.B. was booked to play Bill Graham's Fillmore ballroom in San Francisco. The bus pulled up outside the venue. Noting that the queue was entirely white, B.B. assumed they had the wrong place and instructed the driver to keep looking. Only on the third time round did Bill Graham come out and assure him that this was indeed the right place. B. B. King was finally off the chitlin circuit.

Bobby Rush, a powerhouse in his sixties who favours Elvis Presley-scale belt buckles and buys hair gel by the bucket, is still on that circuit. Pearce's crew rendezvous with his bus and get aboard to see what life is like for those who haven't got a Grammy. Rush plays the upscale descendants of the bars and juke joints of an earlier age. His audience are relatively affluent but still clearly just folks determined on a night out. Rush is an engaging character with the live performer's absence of scruple. This is not a career. It's a job. He does his own negotiation and drives the bus when his man is tired. He gets major build-up prior to his entrance and hits the stage like a man possessed.

Rush's girl singers are built for comfort not for speed. When one turns and speed-rotates her nether parts for the men in the audience the effect is heart-stopping for those brought up on the buff babes of MTV and a reminder of a more jovial age of sexuality.

Rush is looking for the break that means he doesn't have to work so hard. It probably won't come. B. B. King had that break years ago and he still plays 250 nights a year. Here the urge to tour is more than an economic imperative. It's a way of life.

Finally there's Rosco Gordon, a sweet, modest piano player in his seventies who had hits in a jump blues vein in the mid-fifties.

119

One of these was called 'The Chicken'. Gordon's stage act would feature a rooster called Butch who dressed up in suits like his master and was trained to drink whisky. Rosco had moved away from Memphis years earlier to New York to run a laundry business. When his wife died he went back into music. 2002 found him back on Beale Street to take part in a tribute to Sam Phillips at the Handy Awards.

In Pearce's film, Gordon walks the street and wonders why everybody has to play so loud. He combs the racks of a record shop in search of his own music and only comes up with Robert Goulet. In the big Ike Turner-directed jam at the end of the Handy show he is completely at sea and candid enough to admit it but nonetheless thrilled to be on the same stage as B. B. King. Six weeks after the show he died at his home in Queens.

'The Soul of a Man', Wim Wenders' look at the lives of Skip James, Blind Willie Johnson and J. B. Lenoir, and 'Warming by the Devil's Fire', Charles Burnett's personal account of his childhood being shuttled between Los Angeles and Mississippi, both suffer from the lack of living characters like Gordon, Rush and King and opt unconvincingly for actors and soft focus.

The British have been discouraged from taking pride in much these days but there are points in 'Red, White and Blues', the episode about the relationship between blues and British rock in the sixties, when the chest has to be allowed to swell. It's made by Mike Figgis, the director of such movies as *Leaving Las Vegas* and a former musician himself, and features contributions from Eric Clapton, Jeff Beck, Humphrey Lyttelton, Lonnie Donegan, Georgie Fame, Peter Green, Steve Winwood, Chris Barber, Chris Farlowe, Tom Jones, George Melly, Lulu and many others.

The relationship between the music of Memphis and Chicago and the club scenes of West London and the North of England changed the direction of rock music for ever. The sixties generation of British musicians had just enough distance on the blues. They heard it as music rather than a facet of their society with which they were not comfortable and there was something in it that spoke to them. If you were serious about music in the 1960s you tunnelled backwards from the Rolling Stones or John Mayall via Jimmy Reed and Otis Rush to Howlin' Wolf and Robert Johnson. The black and white bag from Dobell's Jazz & Blues Shop in the Charing Cross Road was the mark of a cultured person. People like John Lee Hooker visited the UK and appeared on *Ready Steady Go!* on Friday nights – that's prime time, watched by everybody, not shuffled off into a late-night arts ghetto. It's comparable to the Buena Vista Social Club turning up on *Top of the Pops*.

The contrast between Steve Winwood and his American contemporary Al Kooper, who appears in Scorsese's film, points up the gulf. Kooper, growing up in Newark, knew nothing but the occasional Jimmy Reed hit. Winwood, growing up in Birmingham, and 'more interested in the music than the social change', was singing 'Georgia On My Mind' in the manner of Ray Charles when he was fifteen, long before he ever had the chance to go there.

The memories of these Brits are somehow more impressive than anybody else's in the series of films: George Melly laughing about how Mick Mulligan had to lock his door to escape the secular attentions of Sister Rosetta Tharpe; Peter Green, a man who has had his share of psychiatric problems, happily having no difficulty reeling off the names of the artists on his old *Folk Blues* albums; Eric Burdon wondering at 'the magical structure of those three chords'; Humphrey Lyttelton on how the day the rest of the band didn't turn up led to his hit with 'Bad Penny Blues' which was the inspiration for 'Lady Madonna'; Eric Clapton talking about the pride he takes in the fact that Robert Johnson is now almost a household name. The idea that a Mississippi blues singer was made famous by a boy from Surrey who wasn't even born when he died should give us pause when we catch ourselves thinking that music travels a straight line.

Music moves like water or smoke, defeating the best efforts of the people who make money from it to get it to flow along predictable channels. In 'Godfathers and Sons', Marc Levin's film about the Chicago blues, Marshall Chess, son of Leonard Chess, the Polish Jew who came to the windy city and ended up recording Muddy Waters, Howlin' Wolf, Chuck Berry and Bo Diddley, gets together with Chuck D, guiding spirit of Public Enemy and a man rightly concerned by the fact that we live in a society that has forgotten its past.

Between the contemporary action and the walks down streets that barely exist any more (in the case of 'Godfathers and Sons' it's Chicago's Maxwell Street in the area the blacks used to call 'Jewtown') there is archive footage, much of which is clearly having to be eked out. There's a Bo Diddley recording session from the early sixties. There's the imperious Muddy Waters on stage in the days when his hair rose vertically from his head and he favoured suits you could check your reflection in. There's colour footage of Howlin' Wolf performing, winking at the camera and even talking.

All documentary films need some kind of event to build towards, no matter how spurious, and here it's the reunion of the musicians who played on a record called *Electric Mud* in 1968.

Electric Mud was young Marshall Chess's attempt to catch a psychedelic wave by putting the company's top artist Muddy Waters, the man with the strongest musical personality in the whole of the blues genre, in the studio with a bunch of young guys with wah-wah pedals and electronic keyboards. Blues purists hated it. So did Muddy. (Marshall Chess gets some award for chutzpah for then doing the same with Howlin' Wolf who also hated it. The album was put out under the title 'This is Howlin' Wolf's new album. He doesn't like it. He didn't like his electric guitar at first either.')

But to prove that there is no record so shut away from the love of humanity that it cannot find a defender somewhere, *Electric Mud* impressed the young Chuck D in Long Island. He brings his turntablist Juice to Chicago to take part in the session along with Chicago rapper Common. There's a glorious moment of mutual incomprehension when this young man goes through the racks at the Record Mart and picks out recent blues albums entirely on the basis of the garish clothes the musicians are wearing on the cover. 'See this, man? This is hip hop!' he says excitedly. The elderly owner of the shop promises to find him a copy of Speckled Red's *Dirty Dozens*, one of the musical forebears of rap and hip hop. The glazed look on Juice's face suggests that in the end he's more likely to be persuaded by something with the right camp signifiers than an actual piece of music, no matter how much it may be the root from which hip hop is the fruit.

Life's too short and, as Elvis Costello complained to me recently when I interviewed him, 'People can't hear.' 'The fact that kids today don't know about all this is disturbing,' says Chuck D looking through old Muddy Waters albums from the sixties.

The credits at the end of the various parts of Martin Scorsese's series list the people who have died since contributing to the films: Sam Phillips, Lonnie Donegan, Rufus Thomas, Othar Turner, Rosco Gordon and others. B. B. King soldiers on but when he goes the last of the men who wrote the blues style book will have gone.

There will still be interesting outposts such as Mississippi madman R. L. Burnside and the exotic products of the Fat Possum label. Some musicians will tip their hat in the direction of the blues. Kurt Cobain chose to sing Lead Belly's 'In The Pines' on Nirvana's *Unplugged* performance. The White Stripes' Jack White is a great enthusiast for the delta blues ('the first time I heard it I felt like this was what I had been missing my whole life') and his group have recorded Son House's 'Death Letter' and Robert Johnson's 'Stop Breaking Down'. It's entirely possible that the next big thing could be a bunch of kids building their own world on top of the blues like the Rolling Stones did, but I wouldn't hold my breath. You didn't have to travel very far from the cadences of the sixties to reach the blues. That can't be said today. The arrival of mechanized music (no bad thing in itself) cuts off access to certain chords and ways of saying things. Jack White bemoans the loss of narrative in the great hip hop cut-up. When blues notes find their way into records today they have to be flown in – like the samples of the long-dead Bessie Jones on Moby's album *Play*.

When I went to the Delta in 1978 British pop music was going through one of its more self-regarding periods. It seemed that the blues was slipping over the horizon for good. But somehow it endures. It doesn't change much but we do. We reach an age when we cease believing that it's all about tomorrow. Most of the music that was monopolizing my head in 1978 has fluttered away but the music that was recorded in 1929 in Wisconsin or in 1952 in Chicago looms larger all the time. Like the First World War it assumes fresh importance as it gets more distant.

The survivors die out but the records are still there. If somebody asked me for one of those lists of records I've been listening to this year I would be forced to mention at least ten of the titles listed below. These are not chosen for their antiquity. Music as forceful as this spills into the air, colours the room and lives wholly in the moment. Just this weekend I listened through the crackle and heard, really heard, Charley Patton for the first time.

I honestly don't care whether they do any more of it as long as I can hear what's already been did. Looking back on the history of blues what's remarkable is that it got this far. Without government subsidy or a star system, without media, long before Martin Scorsese or the dawn of the multinational companies who claim ownership of the masters, long before Eric Clapton or Jack White, long before festivals and blues clubs, this fragile weed sank its roots and survived.

By rights it shouldn't be here at all. We shouldn't even be thinking about it. All the more reason to say it. Happy Birthday, the blues.

Ten favourite blues recordings:

Memphis Jug Band: 'K. C. Moan'
B. B. King: 'You Upset Me Baby'
Blind Willie Johnson: 'Dark Was The Night'
Mississippi Fred McDowell: 'Shake 'Em On Down'
Lightnin' Slim: 'Rooster Blues'

Muddy Waters: 'To Young To Know'
Elmore James: 'I Can't Hold Out'
Otis Rush: 'All Your Love'
Richard 'Rabbit' Brown: 'James Alley Blues'
Blind Blake: 'Too Tight'

EVERYTHING I KNOW ABOUT ROCK TV

In early December 1980 I got a call from Mike Appleton. I knew Mike because a few years earlier I'd been working as radio and TV promotion man for the independent label Beserkley. Mike was the producer of *The Old Grey Whistle Test*, which had been the BBC's 'flagship' rock magazine programme since its launch in 1971. Ever since then I had been watching it with my lip curled. This didn't make me uniquely cynical. Most of the people of my acquaintance who reckoned they knew a thing or two about music, who worked in record shops or read the *NME*, might admire the people who were guests on the show but jealously reserved their right to sneer at all the people who put on the show.

When Mike Appleton rang me that day his call wasn't a complete surprise. A week earlier, on a trip to New York, ostensibly to see the Police, I'd managed to get a ticket to see Bruce Springsteen at Madison Square Garden on Thanksgiving. After the show they had a party in the bowling alley in the Garden and I had bumped into Mike there. Emboldened by drink I had told him that he ought to have me as one of the presenters on his programme. Now he was on the phone asking if I could come on the programme and 'do the Christmas books'.

'Doing the Christmas books' was a standard seasonal item for any magazine programme, either on radio or TV, which had any kind of claim to 'doing rock'. In those days the racket of publishing books about music was in its infancy so I wasn't making a choice from the widest selection. Anyway I agreed I would do it, put the date in my recently acquired Filofax, and waited for the standard bike to arrive bearing the books I had to talk about.

The recording took place at Shepperton Studios, because there was no room for us at Television Centre. I don't remember much in the way of detail other than the fact I was ill with nerves before doing the segment, which involved Annie Nightingale, who had been the presenter since Bob Harris left the show in 1978, gently guiding me through the items and ensuring that I didn't make too much of an ass of myself. Following the recording I experienced a level of profound relief which was almost sexual. The best thing about telly, I quickly decided, was the feeling of having just done it.

Nonetheless I wasn't immune to the seductive appeal of being on it again. *Whistle Test* was the only kind of programme that was ever going to ask me to take part. It was the only place on television where you were likely to see the kind of acts that were written about in the *NME* or talked up by the guys who worked in smart record shops. I was one of that generation who made sure I didn't miss the appearances of favourites such as Little Feat, Ry Cooder, Richard Thompson, Tom Waits and Jackson Browne.

In those days *Whistle Test* performed the invaluable service of proving that the people who made the records did in fact actually exist. To hear Ry Cooder's albums was one thing. To actually see him with that handkerchief on his head playing 'Vigilante Man' and accompanying himself on the mandolin, to note the fact that he had a glass eye (which was not the kind of thing that would ever come up in the course of six hundred words in the *Melody Maker*), was suddenly to be brought dramatically closer to him and his world.

The experience of first seeing your heroes on *Whistle Test* in the middle of the 1970s was different in a respect today's TV viewers cannot possibly imagine. This was the only time you were going to see them. As soon as the four minutes of the performance were over it was very unlikely that you would ever get to see John Prine or the J. Geils Band, Harry Chapin or the Sensational Alex Harvey Band, Judee Sill or Crazy Horse, the Climax Blues Band or the Sutherland Brothers and Quiver ever again. There was no home VCR in those days and certainly no YouTube. Once it was gone it was apparently gone.

This was the same no matter how high your status. There's a wonderful clip of George Harrison visiting Granada TV in the late seventies and being taken into an edit suite to be shown an old clip of the Beatles doing 'This Boy' on a 1963 magazine show. He's clearly never seen it before. What's more, it's clear he hasn't seen his old group in a while either. It's very touching to watch him watching himself because in those days it was a rare experience even for a Beatle to be able to retrieve something from what seemed like the distant past.

Hence the *Whistle Test* faithful would lean towards the screen and focus every last bit of their attention on the performance, making sure that they retained every last nuance for immediate replay in the cinema in the back of their heads. They watched the programme with the ferocious concentration of spies being given a secret formula to commit to memory. Then they went to work the following morning and complained about the inadequate words of Bob Harris or Annie Nightingale or whoever happened to be in the presenter's hot seat. This seemed just the natural way of things. I hadn't yet twigged that the viewer's affection for the presenter is in inverse proportion to their own attachment to the subject. Also I hadn't yet absorbed the core truth of all television, which is that the presenter is rarely to blame, but always ends up with all the egg on their face.

In my time as a plugger I'd had occasion to attend the recording of more than one music TV show. The first time I did so I realized another great truth of television: the requirements of the people making the programme will always supersede the requirements of the people they are making the programme about. In 1977 I'd delivered Jonathan Richman and the Modern Lovers to *Top of the Pops*. This experience left me full of admiration for those performers who had managed to overlook the surroundings of the studio – which managed to engender school play levels of inhibition – and project their songs beyond the heads of the technicians and the listless girls the BBC ticket unit had bussed in to reach the viewers at home in their living rooms. The playback Jonathan and his band were expected to mime to in the studio was so quiet you could hear the feet of the audience shuffling on the studio floor.

Whistle Test was different because here the bands played live. Bob and the interviewees might even smoke while talking. I'm sure I attended one recording where there were pints of lager alongside the ashtray on the coffee table. During this period I saw one interview with Keith Richards, an interview that taught me another truth about rock stars and television: the harder they try to look relaxed the more they betray the fact that they're terrified. This certainly applies to Richards whose CGAF act is as considered as Dean Martin's drunkenness or Dolly Parton's chest. On this occasion Keith had arranged himself with one leg crossed over the other. This leg was nervously swinging as he spoke. Every time the leg swung back and forth his boot came into contact with the floor stand on which the microphone was capturing his words. Thus every sentence was metronomically punctuated with the boom of his cowboy boot on the metal. Keith was so deeply engaged in the effort of maintaining his screen of insouciance he didn't know he was doing it and nobody in the studio felt sufficiently empowered to tell him to stop. At the same time nobody in the studio could think about anything else.

And of course – a further truth about television coming up – nobody expects anyone to say anything memorable on television. It's a visual medium. You can get 90 per cent of the messaging content from the average TV programme with the sound turned right down. This certainly applied with *Whistle Test*. The viewers might have been listening to the sound of Keith, looking closely at his physical state of repair and wondering where on earth he got those boots, but they were not expecting much in the way of wisdom from him. (Think about it. All the most memorable quotes from rock stars come from press interviews. Here they've been painstakingly reconstructed by professional writers out of hours of rambling interview tape. For every rock star who can justifiably claim they've been injured by the misrepresentations of journalists there are a dozen who've been made to appear wiser and more articulate by those very misrepresentations.)

'Doing the Christmas books' in December 1980 was my first time in front of a TV camera and therefore my first acquaintance with the feeling of terrible vulnerability and aching self-consciousness that goes with it. If you think your conversational style is smooth, your sentences articulate and that you do not present as a bundle of distracting tics, nervous twitches and involuntary noises, then that simply means you have not yet been on TV. Being on TV is something any idiot can do but only a special handful of idiots can do well. They do it well because to them is vouchsafed the strange gift of being able to look as though they're relaxed when in fact they're in turmoil. The first time I saw myself on television I realized I didn't have this gift.

We were watching at a friend's house. When my segment came on I could only watch it from a position looking round the door from the hallway. I have hardly ever watched myself on TV since. When I am forced to do so I still position myself behind an item of stout furniture. I'm sure I'm not alone in this. The majority of talk show hosts are men. Note how they all position themselves behind a desk. This desk serves no practical purpose. It's there to provide some cover for their genital area, the seat of all their feelings of insecurity.

The segment can't have been a complete catastrophe because

early in the following year Mike Appleton asked me back and suggested I should present a regular slot in the programme called 'Newsdesk'. This would involve me sitting behind a desk, shuffling papers, reading out tour dates and, in May 1981, delivering a kind of obituary to Bob Marley. In those days there were only three channels of television in the United Kingdom and therefore there weren't hundreds of programmes all queuing up to 'do something' on a story like Bob Marley.

Another consequence of there only being three channels of TV was that to be on TV at all was a very big deal. As soon as I started appearing on the programme regularly I joined the company not of the famous, but of the group of people who are mildly well-known among a certain group of people. As soon as I became a regular, any walk down any street was transformed into a kind of moving focus group through which I came to know the kind of people who watched *Whistle Test*.

This was a dedicated minority of people. Live music on television is quite hard work for the viewer. If you don't happen to like the music they're playing – and remember, nothing divides people like music – then most rock bands on TV just look like an unprepossessing bunch of blokes earnestly struggling with heavy machinery. For the casual viewer rock on TV is something that has no fringe benefits. Unlike most TV programmes, where at any given moment half of the audience will be made up of people who were looking for something else but have lingered because the presenter is physically attractive, a programme like *Whistle Test* was only watched by people who were prepared to endure a live set from Robin Trower, Randy California's Spirit or some new band signed to A&M that nobody would ever hear from again, in order to watch two minutes of the new video from ABC over which the credits would inevitably roll. That group of people would therefore be at best a minority of a minority. That was doubly the case back in the days when all television speakers were tiny and tinny and the majority of musicians looked more like Maggie Bell than Beyoncé. Furthermore, a significant number of the viewers were likely to be asleep because in those days television still closed down overnight and therefore *Whistle Test* was sometimes the last thing between the snooker and the disappearing white dot.

I've just consulted the archives and I note that the guests on the programme when I first appeared were Jon Anderson of Yes and Fingerprintz. This kind of pairing was a classic example of *Whistle Test* booking, being an unsuccessful solo offshoot of an off-the-boil supergroup put together with some post-punk hopefuls from Scottish League Division Two. As soon as I began to do the programme regularly, first with Annie, then with Mark Ellen and Andy Kershaw, I was assailed by complaints from fans who wanted to know why their favourite act wasn't on the programme and why this other act that they didn't like or hadn't heard of was. That was because there was a massive amount of politics involved. By the early eighties when I started doing the programme the hotter old acts didn't want to do it because they felt that there was as much to lose as to gain in submitting to a live performance on a programme that was often broadcast live; similarly the hotter new acts often didn't want to do it because they thought it was old hat, and also they weren't confident they were good enough live to come over well.

In order to distinguish the programme from *Top of the Pops* Mike had always insisted that it be fronted by journalists. This at least meant that they could speak their own words rather than having them written by a researcher. The drawback of employing journalists is they like stories. Performers, on the other hand, don't want to be treated like stories. They want to be treated as artists and stars. They do not warm to the idea of being part of a larger narrative. There is nothing more uncomfortable than standing in front of a band and making an amusing point about them. Actually there is. It's doing it again because somebody has made a mistake the first time through. I once introduced Aswad in front of a live audience at the Nottingham Boat Club with what I thought was the quite good line 'harder than this they do not come'. Roar from crowd. Band strikes up. Fifteen seconds later they have to stop and we do the whole thing again. And we do it four times, by which time my line was sounding about as spontaneous as a Theresa May stump speech. This may be why Jools Holland has prospered so long by confining his presenting duties to standing in front of a band, waving his arms around to indicate enthusiasm and restricting his actual opinions about them to the words 'lovely' and 'wonderful'. People love him for it.

The key function of a TV presenter is to be a cheerleader, which places a great deal of importance on there being something worth cheering for. With *Whistle Test* there was a tendency to book acts who looked as though they ought to be good because they slotted into some established tradition but just didn't have the distinctiveness to make it. There is something sad and retrospectively hilarious about being professionally obliged to big up an act that then doesn't make it. It's like John the Baptist repeatedly heralding the wrong Messiah. Trust me. This time. When I look back at the listings of the old programmes from the early eighties and realize that at one time I must have been the person who promised that the world would hear more of Kissing the Pink, Light of the World, Annabel Lamb, Cowboys International or Allez Allez, I feel like a best man who has presided at a series of weddings that all ended in divorce.

Little things stick in the memory. I remember John Martyn and Danny Thompson sniggering at the attempts of Carmel's jazz combo to get their double bass in tune during the run-through. Musicians can be such bitches. I remember when we interviewed Kate Bush in the studio in Manchester she had hired a goods van on the train from Euston so she'd have room to rehearse her dancers. Musicians can get away with things nobody else can get away with. I remember the time Morrissey turned up during one of the Rock Around the Clock marathons with which we marked the bank holiday and was pressed into answering phone calls from viewers wishing to take part in the Video Vote. In those days even Morrissey did as he was told. I remember one studio show where the guests were Marillion and Wah! Musicians like to think they're poles apart when in fact they're blood brothers. In 1985 I remember Harvey Goldsmith coming into the studio to announce the dates for Bruce Springsteen's tour live on the programme, which was a major slap in the face for the print media. I don't recall introducing Fun Boy Three at the Regal Theatre in Hitchin but apparently I did. Thanks to YouTube all these shows live for ever and come back to haunt you.

The most interesting times I had with *Whistle Test* (the 'Old' and 'Grey' were officially dropped from the title during my tenure in a doomed attempt to improve the programme's image) were on those occasions when we went overseas to film interviews. I tended to be the presenter invited to accompany Mike Appleton on these trips. Why did I get the nod? Maybe I'm a quick study. Thanks to Mike I ended up in many places I wouldn't otherwise have found myself. One night I rode the mechanical bull in Gilley's in Pasadena, 'the biggest honky-tonk in Texas'. I spent a strange night in a park in Houston watching as Jean-Michel Jarre illuminated the skyline of the downtown business district during one of his inexplicable cityscape spectaculars. I spent the night in Central Park, back in the days before New York was safe, while Steve Van Zandt shot a scene for a film called *Men Without Women* which, as far as I know, never came out. At Mike's behest I put on an electric blue Bugs Bunny suit for the mild amusement of a class of Japanese children in Tokyo. I went to the Limelight club in New York with U2 at the height of the go-go eighties, feeling like a character from a Jay McInerney book. I seemed to be the only person in this painstakingly desecrated church using the bathroom for its original purpose.

In between all this bacchanalia I was running magazines in the UK and returning to a suburban family life with young children. The week before I was due to fly to Barbados to interview Mick Jagger as part of a programme we were making about the Rolling Stones in 1985 I chose to give up smoking. On the flight over I was popping Nicorette chewing gum tablets with roughly the same regularity I had formerly smoked cigarettes. That's what you did on long-haul flights in those days. When we arrived at the hotel in Bridgetown we went to the bar where Mike insisted we drink rum stingers. The following morning I woke to find that the combination of twenty Nicorettes and a tray of exceptionally strong drinks had conspired to entirely deprive me of my voice. This meant there was no question of me interviewing Mick the following day. The great man was told I had a cold and the interview was postponed for a couple of days during which time we managed to get tickets to see England being spanked by the West Indies in the deciding Test. At one point I found myself sitting next to Mick Jagger in the Sir Garfield Sobers Stand (the sainted Gary himself was sitting a few rows behind) when England batsman Mike Gatting came over to ask Mick whether he would like to join the boys for lunch in the pavilion. Being one of the few people in the world who had achieved sufficient eminence to be able to treat even that invitation as a bit of a bore, Mick apologetically indicated the brown paper package he had just been handed by his personal trainer and said, 'I'm all right, thanks – I've brought my own sandwiches.'

You have to observe a special etiquette around very famous people. It's the custom of Her Majesty the Queen never to say hello or goodbye. You can see why. The former would be superfluous. The latter would be a slight. Being the Queen she is the key element of every human interaction she's involved with. Mick Jagger enjoys similar stature. Everybody who talks to Mick Jagger is thinking the same thing: I'm talking to fucking Mick Jagger. Same with Bob Dylan. And Paul McCartney. It's a very short list.

Bob Dylan always says that when he looks through the window of a bar he sees the people inside enjoying themselves and wishes he could join in. The problem is he knows that once he goes in it will no longer be the same place. That's a fearful burden to carry around. I've entered rooms alongside Mick Jagger. The intensity of attention, curiosity, lust, obsequiousness and envy that's abruptly turned in his direction is quite something. No wonder these people develop a unique way of making their way through the world. Dylan pulls a hood over his head. When I interviewed him he said, 'I could just disappear into a crowd.' Macca walks the streets, responding to every greeting with a cheery thumbs-up but never ever stopping. Mick Jagger's motto is 'give them a glimmer' – hence the working name he and Keith Richards adopted.

Interviewing rock stars on film puts you in the position of having to fake a kind of instant intimacy with them, an intimacy which can't possibly be real because it hasn't passed through the normal stages of friendship. You will know when you're actually friends with a rock star. It will be when the two of you can spend time talking about something other than him. I can count the number of rock stars I have that kind of relationship with on the fingers of one hand. They sometimes say, 'We should go for a drink some time.' They probably think they mean it as they say it but really they don't.

Sometimes it's nice if they go to the trouble of pretending they're your friend. I've interviewed Bruce Springsteen a few times. I spoke to him in Los Angeles in 1992. The first time we spoke that day was for television. Immediately afterwards we went to a quiet room to talk for print. Springsteen finds the process of being interviewed congenial. Maybe he finds it to be a kind of therapy. Hence he talks. And talks. Sometimes he does not know when to stop. For the interviewer two hours is a long time to spend nodding furiously and thinking what you might say next. It drains you. Hence it was me who called a halt to our chat after two hours.

The following day his manager said to me, 'Did you not go for a drive? Bruce was going to take you for a drive.' Hence I missed the opportunity to pretend he was my best mate for an hour.

If musicians think you're a TV personality they treat you as somebody in the same racket they're in. You're not a civilian. You're going to keep their secrets. What goes on tour stays on tour. This is a posture most TV personalities are more than happy to go along with. Since I've always regarded myself as a writer rather than a TV person this has led me into a number of situations where I've been uncomfortably aware of my compromised position.

I was occasionally there when things didn't quite go according to plan, which is the kind of thing that journalists like but film makers don't. I was involved in a film with Level 42 which was supposed to track their triumphal entry into the American market. The minute the album came out it was clear there was going to be no triumphal entry. There was going to be no *Ed Sullivan* moment. This made it far more interesting to me as a writer but there was no chance of any of it being reflected on film. In 1985 I found myself in a conference room at the Rolling Stones office in Cheyne Walk when Mick Jagger was told that Bill Wyman was planning to turn up at their party that night with his new girlfriend who was clearly underage. When I interviewed Springsteen in New York in late 1986 one of the crew told me he was breaking up with his wife. Even had I been able to confirm that, which didn't become a fact for some months, I couldn't write about it. When you're making the film you're part of the show rather than part of the caravan covering the show. And the show always has to end on a high note. TV has triumph in its very DNA, which is why so many programmes build towards the line 'in the nick of time'. Journalism, on the other hand, craves ambiguity.

One of the last things I did for *Whistle Test* was serve as one of the presenters of Live Aid in the summer of 1985. I still stick to my belief that the reason it turned out to be such a success was that for once the English weather did us all a favour. If the sun hadn't shone the pictures wouldn't have been so attractive and the audience wouldn't have grown during the day in the way it did. I remember the heat. I remember the feeling of almost hysterical excitement around the production. At one stage a voice from the production truck came over my earpiece and told me I was about to speak to the largest TV audience ever assembled. This, like most things TV producers say to presenters, is notable for being both impressive and absolutely no help at all.

The climax of my particular shift was the time I was talking to Bob Geldof. He was keen that the broadcast should be a fundraiser. The BBC was keen that this purpose would be secondary. Hence the strict protocol we had to follow every time we gave the audience details of how to donate: postal address first, banks second, credit card line third. Geldof had just finished his most recent round of table banging about the urgency of getting funds to these people. I tried to mollify him by suggesting we should give the appeal details.

'First the address,' I said, knowing what visuals would appear and in what order.

'Fuck the address,' he said in front of the world's largest TV audience and the world's most dismayed TV presenter.

Since that day I have met people all over the world who quote verbatim their memory of what he said. Their memory is always incorrect. I guess that's the way myths work. People construct the reality that matches their dreams.

That was the moment at which the day took off. That was the

instant that set in train the cult of personality that culminated in Geldof's knighthood. That lit the blue touch paper that resulted in people in TV making entire careers on the basis that they had been involved in Live Aid. I can't complain. There are many downsides to being on the TV but the upside is that more people know your name afterwards than before.

What you should never do, however, is overestimate how much they know. Twenty years after Live Aid a magazine sent me to Ethiopia to mark the anniversary. Touring the country it was immediately apparent that while Live Aid had done valuable work, both in raising money and in drawing attention to the crisis, a great deal of the heavy lifting had been done by governments and intergovernmental bodies such as the UN and EU. But nobody remembers them. In Britain it's all the story of one man against the world. Talking to a bunch of farmers in Tigray who had survived the famine, I asked my interpreter, who worked for the relief organizations, to ask them if they had heard of Bob Geldof.

The interpreter turned to me and asked, 'Who's Bob Geldof?'

Let that be a lesson to all of us.

WHY SOME ACTS DON'T MAKE IT

I was listening to an interesting programme about Judee Sill on Radio 4. Sill made a couple of very good albums for Asylum in the early 1970s. She had a song called 'Jesus Was A Cross Maker' that was almost celebrated at the time. Celebrated, at least, among the people who might have watched *The Old Grey Whistle Test* or read the *Melody Maker*. Obviously not mass but better known than most things.

Sill died in 1979. There had been a lot of sadness in her life: drugs, accidents, abuse. When that happens there's always the chance that thirty-five years later Radio 4 will commission a programme about you and it will inevitably be called *The Lost Genius of Judee Sill*.

But here's the thing. When acts make it big they take it as proof of their talent. They did it on their own.

When they don't make it big they always blame it on something or someone specific. The record company went out of business, the radio banned us, the drummer left, there was a strike, there was an oil crisis or a war, there was somebody who had it in for us.

If the artists don't make such a claim then enthusiasts have to make it for them. The story here is that Sill outed David Geffen, the boss of her record company, on stage. In this narrative he had his revenge by dropping her from the label. I'm not sure the record business works like that. It's more likely that his company had put out the two albums they were obliged to release under the terms of Sill's contract, records which hadn't sold. Therefore they decided their money would be better spent on somebody else.

I was talking to Simon Napier-Bell the other night about how performers possess a combination of self-belief and chronic insecurity which you would consider mad if you encountered it in a member of the public. This same egoism drives them to believe that the only thing standing between them and widespread acclaim is some kind of wicked plot. They would rather believe that somebody has been deliberately trying to do them down than to accept the truth, which is that we, the public, weren't really bothered one way or the other. *We're* the villains, not the mythical 'suits' or the tin ears at radio. Our natural state is indifference. We bought some other music or we didn't buy any music at all. We forgot. We passed by on the other side. We have lives in which your career doesn't figure at all.

When we don't buy your record it's nothing to do with you. As the ex-girlfriend would say, it's not you, it's us. But whereas she would be saying it to spare your feelings, we're saying it because it's the brutal truth.

But performers, whose job is the winning of hearts, find this impossible to face. They need to believe there's a conspiracy. It's what keeps them going.

MEMO TO OUR OLD FAVOURITES: IT'S NOT YOU, IT'S US

I t's the challenge for any heritage act. The main competition for your new records comes from your old records. Old fans only have so much bandwidth and they'd rather ease back into the embrace of their old favourite than get used to the unfamiliar shape of the new one.

I recently played the new Donald Fagen album, *Sunken Condos*, alongside *The Nightfly*, his debut solo record from thirty years ago. Some reviews have pointed out the things they have in common: high-concept covers, a song about nuclear dread, one deadpan cover version, lots of playing that sounds like it was hard to do, and a certain set-'em-up-Joe resignation about the delivery.

I doubt the untutored ear could detect which one was the old record and which was the new one, which says something about the last thirty years. Some reviewers think the new one could have done with a little more of one quality and a little less of another. Funny how we treat musicians like chefs, as if they could just pop their record back in the oven for a moment and make it better.

It's difficult to decide why one record works and another doesn't. Some parties are huge fun without anyone trying while others are no fun at all despite everyone trying like crazy. You can't accuse *Sunken Condos* of not making the effort. It probably took more heavy lifting than *The Nightfly*. Maybe it's the absence of catchy tunes that brings its busyness to your attention. It has moments but it never flies in the way that *The Nightfly* did and still does. Only on 'Weather In My Head' does the groove achieve escape velocity. Nothing gets under your skin. It's cold.

The Nightfly, on the other hand, is like a summer evening's drive. Even the songs with quite a bit of plot – 'The Goodbye Look', about a gangster with an appointment with the fishes; 'I.G.Y.', which peers at the future through the binoculars of the year 1957; and 'New Frontier', which is about getting a Tuesday Weld look-alike alone in your dad's fallout shelter – glide by as if on castors. It's one of those cases where the session guys are doing more than the minimum. Each tiny instrumental fill at the end of a line is distinct from the one at the end of the last line. Each one is a new spring driving the watch. *The Nightfly* is one of those records where you don't just sing along with the songs. You play the arrangements with your eyebrows and the drums with your extremities.

But then you would, wouldn't you, because you've lived with it for thirty years. That record is imprinted in you because you've heard it so much. No new record by Donald Fagen or Bruce Springsteen or Tom Petty or anyone else who was making records back in the seventies and eighties is ever going to be listened to as intently as the records that made their names. Elvis Costello still talks passionately about the day he bought Joni Mitchell's *Blue* and took it home to his dad's place in Twickenham where he listened to it so hard he almost took the shine off it. 'I'll never listen to music that way again.'

In his book *The Shallows: How the Internet Is Changing the Way We Read, Think and Remember*, Nicholas Carr argues that the human brain changes all the time and that in recent years the internet has rerouted our neural pathways. I wish he'd do something similar about what repeated exposure to the same music does to us. It must change us. Repeated listening must make us different. The people who heard the first performances of Beethoven's works expected never to hear those works again in their lives. I've heard the great records of Donald Fagen literally thousands of times. I've heard them far more than Donald Fagen will have heard them. (The reason Paul McCartney's backing band can do the Beatles so well is that they've spent thousands of hours listening to Beatles records. Paul McCartney never did.)

Whenever an old favourite releases a new album some of the reviewers want to persuade us the artist has got the old magic back. They always list the familiar ingredients: the choruses, the hooks, the sense of purpose which has apparently returned. The laundry list of qualities is the first refuge of the rock critic who can't really think of anything to say. Lists move in when love moves out. After a while they don't play it any more, which is the one review that really counts. What he should say to his old love is what he's probably found himself saying back in the dim and distant past when other kinds of affairs reached their natural end. It's not you. It's me.

WHEN NOVELISTS WRITE ABOUT ROCK

I was quite enjoying the Jeffrey Eugenides novel *The Marriage Plot* until I came to this sentence: 'Leonard stopped at a gas station with a minimart, where he bought a cassette of Led Zeppelin's Greatest Hits.'

I'm sure I'm not the only reader who had to pause at that point because, as any rock bore would be dying to tell you, there is no such record as *Led Zeppelin's Greatest Hits*. In fact, in 1982, when the novel is set, there were no Led Zeppelin compilations of any kind. So that's just wrong-wrong-wrongity-wrong, the kind of thing that happens when the pursuit of hip leads to the inevitable slip.

Ian McEwan did something far worse in his book *On Chesil Beach* where Edward plays Florence what he calls 'clumsy but honourable' cover versions of Chuck Berry songs by the Beatles and the Rolling Stones. Apart from the wrongheadedness of this critical dismissal of the Beatles' 'Roll Over Beethoven' and the Rolling Stones' 'Come On', both of which are better than the Chuck Berry originals – I'm sorry, Ian, but this is a FACT – the real problem is the novel is very precisely set in July 1962, which was a year before either of those groups had got round to recording Chuck Berry songs.

Then there's simple knowledge overreach. In *Norwegian Wood*, Haruki Murakami writes: 'she performed a few Bacharach songs next: Close To You, Raindrops Keep Falling On My Head, Walk On By, Wedding Bell Blues.'

At which point you put your hand up and say, 'But surely, Mr Famous Writer, "Wedding Bell Blues" was written by Laura Nyro and not Burt Bacharach. If you weren't sure, why mention it?'

Sometimes these minor gaffes can be corrected in later editions. Though Ian Rankin, who does know a lot about music, was so mortified about having attributed the song 'I Can See Clearly Now' to Marvin Gaye rather than Johnny Nash in his novel *Black & Blue* that he insisted it be left. This seems unnecessarily noble of him.

Do these kind of mistakes matter? Well, no, but also well, yes. There's a certain kind of topical reference you can get away with in a modern novel. You can allude to prime ministers or current affairs and very few readers will check your working out. But there are two areas best steered clear of: one is football and the other is pop music. They're both too particular, somehow too real, too much part of a reader's personal hinterland. It's like suddenly reading your own phone number in the middle of a piece of fiction. You're jerked out of the fictional world of the narrative and into the real world of your front room where the same record may be sitting.

However, the writer can't resist mentioning it because he – and it almost always is a he – can't resist inviting you round to look at his records or telling you what team he supports. He surrenders to that most dangerous impulse, the need to be liked.

When male authors are trying to get you to identify with their hero they often have him go home to his pit of a flat, uncork a bottle of his favourite Australian red and then reach for a favourite record – which is usually by someone difficult to argue with like Van Morrison, Marvin Gaye, Johnny Cash, Nick Cave or Miles Davis. At which point I feel like telling him not to be pompous and asking if he's got any Kylie.

Finally, it's even more disturbing if they try to mix real music with the fictional kind. Jonathan Franzen got away with it with his alternative rock hero in *Freedom*. Not everyone does. The sentence in *The Marriage Plot* I found most disturbing went as follows: 'They saw Nazareth, Black Sabbath, Judas Priest and Motordeath, a band whose shows featured naked women performing animal sacrifices.'

You're probably wondering why Motordeath's rather extreme live presentation has never brought them to your attention, or indeed that of the local health and safety people. That's because Motordeath didn't exist. If there was a niche for such a group then somebody would have started one. That's the thing about heavy metal and in fact all pop music. You really can't make it up.

IN PRAISE OF WIMPS

I know this is a strange thing to say about a healthy young man who seems to be successfully persuading some of the most attractive young women on earth to pop their clothes off and get into bed with him, only stopping occasionally to check his bank balance, but you have to feel sorry for James Blunt.

The rise of his big hit 'You're Beautiful' to worldwide prominence was accompanied, inevitably in his home country, by a swelling chorus of disapproval. His surname, with its rich potential for rhyming slang, rolled off the tongue of every university-educated would-be regular bloke stuck for a laugh line on a panel show as he found himself unanimously elected the nabob of naff. Of course, his critics were encouraged in their slander by the fact that he is evidently a bit posh and was in the army, and therefore fair game. The same people have yet to be caught observing that the

Gallagher brothers are a bit common. In the British class system you're only allowed to sneer in an upwards direction.

The capital charge against Blunt was that he was a wimp. It seems odd to reflect that before the word 'wimp' became common currency in this country – and I don't remember hearing it until the seventies, when it arrived on our shores along with those other terms of abuse such as 'dork' and 'gonzo' that rock critics spray around with gay abandon – nobody thought of pointing out any of the qualities of oversensitivity or weakness with which it is associated.

If they had they could as easily have pointed out that Scott Walker was certainly a wimp, as were Marc Bolan, David Bowie, Tim Buckley, James Taylor, Jackson Browne and half the most favoured names of the era. Then there would be all the other people who clearly had a sensitive side. Nobody accused the Beatles of being wimpy because of 'Here, There And Everywhere' or suggested that Bob Dylan was going a bit soupy because of 'Lay Lady Lay'. Maybe that's because the advertised distaste for sensitivity, sentimentality, romance, hearts and flowers, call it what you will, only became the rule in the 1970s. It happened, oddly enough, just as life for most people was getting more comfortable and prosperous. In times of war, crisis, loss or deprivation, people have no trouble latching on to sentimental songs because, like it or not, they give voice to some of the things they're feeling. On the other hand, give them peace and prosperity and they start listening to *OK Computer*.

We are all sentimental creatures by nature and the British, though they will stoutly deny it, are actually more sentimental than most. The stiff upper lip has been loose and flabby for years.

For instance, we are now the world leaders in crying at sporting events. You can't move on the pitch at the end of a cup final for toddlers in replica shirts being held high. What's Bob Dylan's most popular song after all these years? 'Forever Young'. What do Oasis always have to play? 'Wonderwall'. The jugular vein of popular music is sentiment. Go and look at all the singles that have remained at number one for extended periods. 'I Will Always Love You'. 'My Heart Will Go On'. '(Everything I Do) I Do It For You'. 'Angels'. They're all vastly sentimental ballads into which people, regular people, find it easy to cast themselves. I'm sorry, Morrissey, this is what most people feel does say something to them about their lives.

The only people who don't happily link arms and join the rest of the nation in a damned good wallow are men like us. Blokes who feel they know a thing or two can tell when the strings are being tugged and aren't bloody well going to fall for it. Because falling for it would seem like going along with the herd. It's a form of snobbery. We don't wave our scarves or raise lighters aloft. We don't sway with the masses. That delicious sensation of allowing these feelings to well up and flood out of us is something we have to force ourselves to surrender to, so well have we inoculated ourselves against its rising gorge.

So there's nothing more irrelevant than what we think of James Blunt, a man who has prospered by tapping into the little-known fact that most women like to be told that they're beautiful. And we should note and inwardly mark the fact that time has a habit of making even the sugariest record acquire a patina of poignancy. Listen to the Flamingos' 'I Only Have Eyes For You' on the soundtrack of *American Graffiti*. Watch John Cusack holding his boom box aloft to play Peter Gabriel's 'In Your Eyes' to his girl-friend in *Say Anything*. Listen to Elvis singing 'Can't Help Falling In Love'. Or Cat Stevens' 'Father And Son'. I could go on but I think I have something in my eye.

WHY MUST EVERYTHING BE DARK AND EDGY?

I ran into a film buff just recently. He promised me the new version of *Superman* is going to be 'quite dark'. The panel on *Late Night Review* have just described a new film of Peter Pan as 'very dark'. Sir Peter Hall will probably be miffed about this because only yesterday on Radio 4 I heard him promising that his upcoming production of *As You Like It* was also going to be 'very dark'. This was in the same programme that a breathless fan of old science fiction had pointed out that the original Godzilla films were 'incredibly dark'.

Observing the beginnings of a pattern here, I did what every self-respecting journalist does these days when he smells a story. I went directly to Google and typed in the words 'actually very dark', and lo what riches poured forth. The following are just a few of the things which have been described as 'actually very dark' (and don't you love the hint of 'where've *you* been?' in that 'actually'?): *Batman*, the ending of *Star Wars*, *Spiderman*, the love songs of U2, Harry Potter, the music of Dar Williams and, I kid you not, *Babe: Pig in the City*.

Flushed with this success I then tapped in 'edgy remake', another one of those approving contemporary catch-alls that shows up regularly in quotes on movie posters. Bingo! I read that Jonathan Demme's *The Manchurian Candidate* is an edgy remake, as was Tim Burton's *Planet of the Apes*, the Coen Brothers' *The Ladykillers*, the recent American film *The Ring* and Gerald Levert's version of an old Bobby Womack song. I also note with some trepidation that New Line Cinema are promising 'an edgy remake' of *The Texas Chainsaw Massacre*. Moving on to 'stylish remake' I found that *Dawn of the Dead* was thus hailed, as were *The Italian Job*, *Alfie*, *The Thomas Crown Affair*, *Ocean's Eleven* and bags more.

'Dark', 'edgy' and 'stylish' have become the default settings on the critical microwave, the three key labour-saving clichés of the contemporary typist. You can see their appeal. 'Dark' is an easy-to-spell adjective that saves you having to reach for more specific adjectives which might characterize the exact nature of the darkness. (I am assuming here that even at its darkest *Babe: Pig in the City* is not operating on quite the same blasted extremity of human experience as, say, *King Lear*.) 'Edgy' will do for describing anything with swearing in it. 'Stylish' is what you call things featuring Jude Law. Add Nicole Kidman and you can make that 'stylish and sexy'. In fact, some of the most vacuous entertainment experiences of recent times have been hailed as 'dark, edgy, stylish and sexy'. We have reached a point where these four adjectives between them are seen as describing the natural condition of art. I suppose there's something in that. Where our parents might have regarded entertainment as primarily there to be light and diverting, we now flatter ourselves that we can take any amount of dark and edgy. To which one is forced to ask, where are the films and books and records about really dark and edgy subjects such as the jihadist Abu Musab al-Zarqawi and the other monsters prowling the perimeter of our mental multiplex?

At the same time we have been sold the idea that seriousness equals substance. Take *John Lennon Acoustic*, a new compilation whacked together for the Christmas market. By focusing on Lennon's supposedly dark and edgy side through the likes of 'Working Class Hero', 'My Mummy's Dead' and 'Woman Is The Nigger Of The World', it provides an object lesson in how the pursuit of gravitas can bring even the greatest talents low. Taste makers who couldn't hear the genius in the middle eight of a Beatles pop song like 'No Reply' were only too happy to overlook the melodic poverty of later Lennon music because it was 'saying something'. The main reason why the Beatles remain, if anything, underrated is because their songs were primarily expressions of their delight in being alive. This kind of simple happiness makes critics uncomfortable. Tragically one of the people most prone to this blind spot was John Lennon himself.

Dark and edgy should be given the rest of the decade off. Instead we should go right to the other end of the spectrum and make a point of exalting those people who have turned dancing in the light into an art form. We should establish a public holiday and raise our glasses to Steely Dan, P. G. Wodehouse, the Temptations, the Beach Boys, Bill Bryson, Nick Lowe, Frank Capra, the Jackson Five, Ian Carmichael, Fred Astaire, Abba, Madness, Hugh Grant, Steve Martin, Peter Kay, the Finn Brothers and anybody else who ever simply gave wings to our delight. Their achievements weigh every bit as heavily as those of a Radiohead, an Irvine Welsh, a Quentin Tarantino or any of the other peddlers of stylish gloom. The only dark and edgy thing, after all, is a hedgehog.

THE PROFOUND JOY OF GETTING RID OF STUFF

We've been in this house twenty-five years this summer. Most of that time has been devoted to raising a family. We didn't pay much attention to the rising tide of stuff we were surrounding ourselves with during that time.

After a while even books, records, DVDs and magazines cease to be the things you worked to acquire. You get to a point where it's either you or the stuff. By that time you've probably had the melancholy experience of clearing the homes of your own parents, people who didn't accumulate a fraction of the junk you've got yourself. You kid yourself you're going to pass on your records to your kids. Then they grow up and you realize that even if they were bothered there's no way their lives could also find room for the detritus of yours.

What do you get rid of and what do you keep? The reasons you once collected things no longer hold good. Spotify and iTunes have made a nonsense of all those compilations you hung on to because of one track. IMDb makes those fat film and TV reference books look ridiculous. Those launch issues of classic magazines you squirrelled away are never going to make you rich but they will attract dust and mildew. You no longer believe that if you pass up one particular CD you will never be able to replace it.

Chucking stuff away is a learning experience. You realize nobody is remotely bothered about the thousand-pound computer you take down the tip. They just point you to the pile in the corner. On the other hand they don't know what to make of the old tea chests because they've never seen one before and you wonder whether you should take them home and hang on to them. You visit the second-hand book store so often that you start to develop an attraction to old paperbacks and find yourself picking up the odd one as you drop off the odd box of fifty.

The process of sifting is slowed down by the occasional piece of paper that flutters out of an old book. A child's hand-drawn birthday card, a note of apology for some long-forgotten breakage, a rejection letter from a job you don't remember applying for, all put away nowhere in particular because somebody thought it would be a shame to lose them. Maybe this was the occasion that you were saving them for. Is anyone really going to pause in the middle of cleaning up to look at them again? Anything that's not been disturbed in the last twenty-five years is, for obvious reasons, unlikely to be disturbed in the next quarter of a century.

Your reward for having got rid of all this stuff is the liberation of the space you need to be able to enjoy the stuff you're left with. The records you can suddenly put your hand on, the newly cleared window seat which you can use as a place to read, the profound calm that steals over you when your desk is finally cleared. This is every bit as spiritual as the impulse that led you to acquire the stuff in the first place.

5
FOR THE LOVE OF RECORDS

When I was young the one thing I wanted was to be near records. When as a young adult I discovered it was theoretically possible to get a job where you could get records either cheap or for free, my ambition was clear. I subsequently exchanged a job in a record shop for a job working in music magazines from which you would come home every night with new records. Unsurprisingly this tended to make a person blasé. Nevertheless I have never got over the excitement of holding a new release in my hands. Nor have most artists, which is why they continue to make albums for which there is very little demand out there in the market.

Over the last ten years, as 'physical product' has passed away and the shops that used to sell them have disappeared from our streets, something has gone out of our lives and all the Record Store Days in the world cannot call it back again. These next few pieces are not about the music. They're about records as products and the important part they used to play in our lives. They used to be hard to find and expensive to buy. Hence we valued them. Now they're impossible to escape and effectively free. Hence we don't.

I HAVE MEASURED OUT MY LIFE IN RECORD SHOPS

'd been working quite hard the other day and felt I needed to take what the health and safety people call a 'screen break'. It was only when I went outside and walked around in the part of London where I work that I realized that I could no longer do the thing I used to do when I had time to kill in any British town or city. I could no longer go into a record shop. Because there weren't any.

I didn't particularly want to buy a record. And I didn't want to ask the advice of some supercilious anorak. Of all the things that I find unconvincing about people's nostalgia for record shops the idea of the helpful older brother figure behind the counter is, in my experience, the most far-fetched. I used to be one of those people and I know how snooty we could be.

I didn't want to buy. I simply wanted to do what I've done so many times over the years, which is kill time in a record shop.

I think I've been this way since I was about ten years old. I'm sure I'm not the only one. When I was young I had no interest in any other form of shopping. Most of the time I wasn't shopping at all in the sense of buying things.

In the days of vinyl I'd stand there and flick through the twelve-inch LPs, reading the sleeve notes and credits on records I knew I would never hear, let alone buy. I would spend entire days in the West End of London 'visiting' everywhere from Harlequin to One Stop to Contempo to Cheapo Cheapo to Dobell's on the Charing Cross Road. I came back empty-handed most of the time but with a head full of stimulation. I fear it's true to say that I learned more in record shops than I did in school. Set me down in even the tiniest town in those days and I would find the best-stocked record shop and be able to compile a mental inventory of the place within ten minutes.

I was reminded of this the other day while looking at a website called the British Record Shop Archive. It won't win any prizes for design but it'll get the vote of anyone who thinks it's important to remember that there once was a tiny record shop in Baker Street station; that M. Hurst of Melton Road, Leicester once sold records as well as 'everything electrical'; and that Earth Records in Aylesbury, Bucks promised that if you came in there with your afghan coat you wouldn't be bothered by what they called 'straights'. I close my eyes and I can summon the different smell of each and every one of them.

I wonder if anyone will miss the vanishing bookshops of Britain as much as the visitors to this site are clearly missing these vanished record shops. Maybe like me they're recalling the long-lost lunch hours, the afternoons bunked off school, the furtive, slightly racy pleasures that only half an hour in a record shop could properly afford. The best record shops were like a cross between an art gallery and a bookie's. Faintly disreputable as well as improving – a potent combination.

Was I alone in being able to achieve a state of inner peace when surrounded by records that I couldn't get anywhere else? Some people went into empty churches, libraries, parks or museums for the same feeling. Some people stared out to sea. For me it was the record shop every time. Some people measured out their lives in coffee spoons. My generation did the same thing in Various Artists A–D. And now it's all gone. Killing time will never be the same again.

REARRANGING THE DECKCHAIRS ON THE SS *RECORD SHOP*

I once worked for HMV. That's not the only reason I wish them luck in the initiative that began three weeks ago with the transformation of their record shop in Dudley into 'a compelling multi-channel social shopping space and experience'. Here customers are encouraged to pass their time drinking smoothies at the Lovejuice Bar, playing games in the Xbox zone, checking their Facebook pages on the computers provided, downloading video clips to their memory sticks and, presumably, even buying a record or two.

Time will tell whether this project will take wing or join the junkyard of retail concepts that have subsided into the chasm between the artist's impression and the Monday morning reality. If it succeeds then Richard Branson will be kicking himself for offloading his Virgin megastore chain at the wrong time and the principals of FOPP, Tower and Music Zone will be grinding their teeth at the riches that could have been theirs had they just held out a few months longer.

The reasons for the decline of the music chains over the last five years are diverse; anyone who thinks they have a simple solution to their problems is merely showing their ignorance. Retailing records is not what it was. These days the supermarkets take the cream by discounting the platinum sellers; much of the music produced by record companies is pumped full of steroids and rendered void of charm in order to get it on the radio; the CD as an item is difficult to love; and now e-tailers like Amazon provide a direct line from your loft into bottomless inventory – particularly bad news for the megastores whose range was always at the heart of their appeal. 'I've got the one you're looking for,' said Nipper the HMV dog in one long-lost TV campaign. Bad news, mutt-face. So do all the other dogs.

Given the choice, HMV wouldn't have chosen to start their journey from here, lumbered with 237 stores in high-street locations increasingly dominated by charity shops and building societies. I'm probably not in the crosshairs of any marketeer but I don't believe I'm alone in thinking that big is no longer beautiful in any form of retailing; not clothes, not food, and certainly not music. At some point in the nineties we crossed an invisible frontier between the plenty that intoxicates and the surfeit that leaves us jaded. The idea of a record store that stocks everything is now about as appealing to me as a pub that stocks five hundred single malts or a restaurant serving both Chinese and Italian food.

Today's most admired retail operations are places like the Apple Store, Top Shop and Nike Town. These brand cathedrals celebrate the things they sell. It's impertinent to mention the things they don't. You wouldn't go into Top Shop seeking sensible shoes, nor expect Apple to fix your Compaq laptop. By the same token you probably wouldn't go into Rough Trade East, the new indie flagship near London's Brick Lane, expecting them to stock the latest winner of *The X Factor*. However, the forty-plus Rough Trade shopper of today will be able to steer his baby buggy between the racks, which was not a consideration when Geoff Travis opened his first shop in the mid-seventies. Let's not be fooled. These people are every bit as cute in targeting their changing audience as the big retail consortiums and one size no longer fits all.

Personally, I dream of a record shop along the lines of my favourite bookshop, Daunt in London's Marylebone High Street. The thing that everybody agrees about Daunt is it's a beautiful environment. Their publicity always leads with this rather than their range or the prices. Inside it's like the library of an Edwardian grammar school and the books seem to have been chosen to complement the ambience. Because I am as much of a snob as most Englishmen, I am also attracted by the other customers, many of whom are older and better dressed than I am. This I find profoundly reassuring. I rarely go there to find anything in particular but I never come out empty-handed.

Record shops were once about urgency. They sold quickly to encourage us to buy quickly. If you came upon something for the first time you could panic yourself into buying it just in case it was the only copy they had and it went out of stock. Music buyers are no longer quite so sheeplike. We know that everything is now here for ever. The relationship between the shop and the customer has changed profoundly. It used to be a breathless clash of tongues in the minutes before the last bus left, and we all know how that can have its own special excitement. In the new world of retail it's all about seduction. The retailers are lowering the lights and artfully arranging their cushions. The question is, will we come in for a cup of coffee?

THE LAST MEGASTORE

I bought a record of tunes Bryan Ferry wrote for the movie of *The Great Gatsby* today in the closing-down sale at the big HMV near Oxford Circus. It's the saddest I've ever felt in a record shop. They were literally taking the place apart as I was shopping.

In the basement the Classical department is long gone, absorbed into the Jazz department, which in itself doesn't seem as big as it used to be. The shrinking of even these specialist departments means this is structural; if it's happening with Classical and Jazz you can't blame the decline of the CD business on *The X Factor*.

I passed the rack of Spoken Word recordings and thought, I bet that lot doesn't resurface in the new store down by Bond Street. I've been there, and it seems to be aimed at selling records to tourists, which no doubt makes sense.

When I worked at HMV, which is forty years ago, it made most of its money selling the hits of the day, just as it does today, but it also prided itself on its curatorial role, on the fact that it stocked the records other record shops had never heard of.

Here there was an International department long before anyone had come up with the term 'world music'. Elsewhere you could get LPs of train noises, stereo test records, EPs of nursery rhymes, Hoffnung at the Oxford Union, BBC sound effects, Count Ossie and the Mystic Revelation of Rastafari pressed on extra-heavy vinyl, military band music from Stalinist dictatorships, *Songs Of The Humpback Whale*, records for self-hypnosis, and even some that went round at sixteen revolutions per minute.

When there was a record business there was always something interesting going on in the margins of the record business. Records that were made because there was a tiny market, records which catered for some special interest group, and records which did OK by selling in tiny quantities, worldwide, for ever. Records which came out because somebody somewhere wanted to put out a record with their name on, something they could hold up and say, 'There, there it is, this is what I did.'

The Ferry record is a classic example of that. There is nothing quite so self-indulgent as Bryan Ferry putting his name on a record of Roxy Music tunes done in the idiom of 1920s jazz. I scoffed as much as anyone when *The Jazz Age* came out and didn't take any notice of the odd review that said, actually, this is quite good. It's taken a few years to find a way into my heart.

Nobody's going to get behind a record like this. No DJ's going to shout about it from the rooftops. It won't produce a hit single. Like so much good music it was thrown a lifeline by Hollywood, when Baz Luhrmann heard it and asked Ferry to provide some music for his soundtrack of *The Great Gatsby*. The 'Jazz Age' hasn't happened yet and it may not but, even a few years ago, it was just conceivable that a record like that could move out of the margins and temporarily lend its spice to the mainstream.

It happened before for records like *Buena Vista Social Club*, *Le Mystère Des Voix Bulgares* and *Missa Luba*. When I was at HMV people would approach the counter with a piece of paper and a 'you won't have heard of this' look on their face. If you told them they were the fifth person to ask for it that day you'd be spoiling their fun. They needed to feel they were free spirits.

In the end it happened for these records and quite a few others because they were records, briefly precious objects as well as means of delivery, tangible monuments to the self-esteem of the people who made them and bought them. The music on them was made because somebody wanted to make a record, not a recording. Nobody's going to go to that trouble to get something on Spotify. Watching them take down the old HMV today I was more than ever convinced that it will take a lot of the record business with it, and maybe the area at the margins is the bit it will take. If there's nowhere to sell records like that, why would you bother making records like that?

NOBODY EVER ASKED A GIRL BACK TO LISTEN TO THEIR ITUNES

Dave Marsh's 1989 book *The Heart of Rock and Soul* is one of the books about music that you need to read. It's a simple idea. Marsh lists his pick of 'the 1,000 greatest singles ever made' and pays tribute to the things that made them powerful.

At the very end of the book is record 1,001. It's 'No Way Out' by Joyce Harris, a tune which, according to Marsh, first surfaced in 1960 and had since circulated on tape among connoisseurs. When I first read the book, twenty years ago, I half-fancied that Marsh had invented Joyce Harris in order to illustrate a greater truth about our love of music.

As he says, 'We're men, not dogs, and when we find a mystery, our job is to solve it, not roll in it . . . Pursuit is half the joy of this line of work.' I was fascinated with the idea that a single side cut long ago by an otherwise uncelebrated artist could embody the heart of rock and soul as well as 'I Heard It Through The Grapevine', which was the first single listed in the book.

Two decades after the book's publication you can find out all there is to know about Joyce Harris and her single by simply googling her name. This does not make me any happier. To me, the fact that Marsh carried a torch for the record was far more interesting than the record itself. Pursuit was half the joy of accumulating records but it is a pleasure that's quietly slipping away from us. Digital music has lots of things to recommend it but its arrival has denied us many pleasures that are essentially senseless but tell us a lot about the fact that we're men not dogs.

Here I'm talking about more than the little signifiers that crop up when old heads are sitting around talking about the glory days of vinyl. I mean the bigger things which measure the hold recorded music once had on the public's heart. I don't think it matters much that you can't roll a joint on an MP3 but I do believe that the demystification of pop music can be directly attributed to the decline of the twelve-inch album sleeve. It doesn't bother me that you can't make an ashtray out of an old CD but I am forcibly struck by the fact that nobody has given a hoot about record labels since records stopped having labels.

We love the sound of music as much as we ever did but our emotions are no longer triggered by proximity to the vessels that carry it. We, dear reader, are the last bunch of people to be able to understand how stirred we were by those vessels. Soon those feelings will be gone from our culture entirely. Even my children don't remember what it was to be given a record for Christmas, to open the parcel with trembling hands, to find it contained the desired album and then to spend the rest of the day playing it, daring it to wear out its welcome. An iTunes token is all very well but it cannot delight the heart like the gift of the record did.

You can't own a download. You merely pay for the legal right to access it. And if you don't own it you can never feel the sensations associated with ownership: envy, desire, longing, touch, nostalgia, the whole nine yards. I find it difficult to imagine that today's seventeen-year-old wants records the way I used to want records. I remember being very conversant with hundreds of records I had never heard, let alone bought. If today's seventeen-year-old had that kind of Jones for music he would satisfy it by digitally acquiring them, legally or otherwise. And is there anything quite as disappointing as having your heart's desire satisfied that easily? It immediately stops being your heart's desire and becomes just another minor gratification. When I was that age the only things I really wanted were records. If you'd taken away my desire for them I don't know how I would have remained motivated enough to get up in the morning.

And while we're talking of desire, I remember a time when the ownership of a bunch of records was one of the few acceptable reasons a young man could provide which might encourage a young woman to visit his dwelling place. There was a time when you could say, 'Come and hear my Van Morrison album' without risking pull-the-other-one derision. No matter how puny a young man's record collection it was also his life story, his diary and a treasure map showing the whereabouts of his often unspoken sensitivities. It was his heart, in fact. No longer.

6
HEPWORTH'S
ROCK LISTS

TEN GREAT ACCIDENTAL TRILOGIES

The 2012 release of a trilogy of albums by Green Day had me pondering the eternal wisdom of Louis Menand's Iron Law of Stardom (that the public can't maintain its enthusiasm for a particular artist much longer than three years) and thinking about the number of acts that made trilogies without meaning to. They're the after-the-fact trilogies, made because the standard record contract used to be for three albums, three years seeming to be as long as you could hold a particular line-up of a band together, as Menand pointed out. It's interesting to go back and look at record-making not as a steady string of albums but as a blind stumble towards a three-album purple patch. Like these.

1. Scott Walker's trilogy of hit albums which came out between 1967 and 1969. Purists disagree, but I think Scott hit his peak with

these three LPs, each of which contained throbbing versions of Jacques Brel compositions like 'Amsterdam' and a sprinkling of his own songs. The next album, *Scott 4*, was all his own songs. It was deleted from the label's catalogue within a year.

2. *Rubber Soul*, *Revolver* and *Sgt. Pepper's Lonely Hearts Club Band* make up a kind of psychedelic triptych, although the word was unknown for most of the period during which they were made. They were just pop records made the best way the Beatles knew how to make them at the time.

3. Bowie fans refer to *Low*, *'Heroes'* and *Lodger*, the three records made between 1977 and 1979, as his Berlin Trilogy, even though the third one wasn't recorded in Berlin. It might be more accurate to call it his Brian Eno trilogy. They've certainly got a unity of mood about them.

4. Between 1973 and 1975 Neil Young made three albums – *Time Fades Away*, *On The Beach* and *Tonight's The Night* – which you could call his ditch trilogy. ' "Heart Of Gold" put me in the middle of the road,' he said. 'Travelling there became a bore so I headed for the ditch.' The story goes that Irving Azoff joined his management on the night he debuted 'Tonight's The Night' by playing the whole harrowing album for an audience expecting the hits. He then came back and encored with the same song. When he came off again Azoff suggested that when he went back he should play something the audience knew. He smiled, went out and played the same song again.

5. Stevie Wonder's pop/soul trilogy starts with 1972's *Talking Book*, his second album of that year, which he followed with

Innervisions the following year and *Fulfillingness' First Finale* the year after that. That's 'Superstition', 'You Are The Sunshine Of My Life', 'Living For The City', 'Boogie On Reggae Woman', 'You Haven't Done Nothin'' and lots more written, recorded and released in a dizzying two years.

6. It's a tragic fact that Nick Drake's enduring legacy is guaranteed by the fact that he never recorded again after his third album and died two years later. 1969's *Five Leaves Left* is a finding-his-feet debut, 1971's *Bryter Layter* was an optimistic attempt to reach a broader market, and the last one, *Pink Moon*, sounded as though he was reconciled to failure. But they're all unimprovable.

7. The Cure made *Seventeen Seconds*, *Faith* and *Pornography* between 1980 and 1982. They didn't set out to make a dark trilogy but when they listened back, they had done.

8. The singer on the first Steely Dan album was David Palmer so that doesn't really count, but the next three – *Countdown To Ecstasy*, *Pretzel Logic* and *Katy Lied*, which were made between 1973 and 1975, when Donald Fagen was the singer – certainly do.

9. You might call the three albums Bob Dylan put out between 1997 and 2006 – *Time Out Of Mind*, *Love And Theft* and *Modern Times* – his geezer trilogy. Here he relaunched himself as a wheezy old gimmer doing retreads of old R&B tunes he'd picked up while doing his *Theme Time Radio Hour*.

10. To my mind the greatest of all the trilogies is Nick Lowe's so-called Brentford Trilogy, which started with 1994's *The*

Impossible Bird and carried on with *Dig My Mood* and *The Convincer*. Nick's alone among rock stars in being better in his sixties than he was in his twenties and finding his senior years more inspirational than his time as a freshman.

TWELVE GREAT SONGS

Wordsworth is our best-known poet. How many of his verses can you call to mind? The one about the daffodils, maybe the one composed upon Westminster Bridge, or the one he made up near Tintern Abbey; if you studied him at school you probably also know 'The Prelude' and a few more. If you could name a dozen of his poems I'd consider you pretty cultivated. Try the same exercise with T. S. Eliot. *The Waste Land*, 'The Love Song of J. Alfred Prufrock', *Four Quartets*, 'Ash Wednesday' and the ones about the cats. Coleridge? *The Rime of the Ancient Mariner*, 'Kubla Khan', 'Frost at Midnight', 'The Nightingale', and then I bet you're struggling.

I mention this because I was reading the diaries of the playwright Simon Gray recently and he said that no man should expect to be able to write more than twelve poems in a lifetime. The poet would probably pen more than twelve in his life, but he shouldn't expect more than a dozen of them to be remembered. Since I read that I've been feverishly checking how the major poets stack up against Gray's dictum. My research underlines that it doesn't matter whether they wrote hundreds or a handful; they'll be lucky if they came up with a dozen poems that you could call hits.

Let's move this thinking into another field. As a unit of creative currency a poem is roughly comparable to a song. If our greatest poet wrote no more than a dozen poems that outlived him, isn't it likely to be the case that our best contemporary songwriters aren't going to leave behind them much more than an average Greatest Hits collection? This may be an affront to your devoted inner fan and you may be thinking that your particular favourite songwriter has actually written scores of memorable songs, but if you conduct a sober audit you'll find that only in the rarest cases does anyone rack up more than the dozen.

I have tested this on the songwriters I most admire. Randy Newman's *Best Of* came out twenty-three years ago and, while I like quite a few records he's made since then, I can't honestly think there's anything that I would take 'Sail Away' off to make room for. Even Stevie Wonder, who's been at this coalface since 1961, could be summed up in a list of twelve. Try this on any of your favourites. Go to their Greatest Hits, lose the half-dozen tracks that have been put on there because they're from the album they'd most recently released, and if you like replace them with the many smashes they've made since. Difficult, isn't it? Because generally speaking they haven't made any smashes since. A Greatest Hits collection isn't just a cash-in. It's also a tacit recognition that the well has gone dry.

Of course there are exceptions. A handful have managed to sustain their creativity beyond the traditional burst that occurs in their late twenties. Bob Dylan is one. Equally, there are people whose short bursts were more productive than most. Burt Bacharach, the Beatles and Paul Simon could all be deemed to have written more than twelve classics but their total doesn't amount to more than, say, twice that number. It makes sense. How many times can you reasonably expect to dip your bucket and have it come up full of jewels? If Wordsworth couldn't manage it, why should Elvis Costello? Of course the record business, by handing out generous contracts to those who have sold records in the past, behaves as if this is not the case, as if quality and success are evenly distributed throughout a performer's career and the hits will continue. They aren't and they won't.

The whole business of being a fan flies in the face of the same logic. A fan's admiration is rooted in what was achieved in the past rather than what is being achieved at the present time. It's like supporting most football teams. This doesn't mean that everything the artist produces beyond the twelve tracks is not worthwhile. You may get hours of pleasure listening to songs written and recorded long after that brief period of inspiration during which the artist first established himself. But they are generally echoes of the real thing rather than the real thing itself. There are the ones you like because they came straight after the good ones or the ones that remind you of their great ones. They're the footnotes, the afterwords, the necessary accompaniment to a career, the reason to go out and play and a way of reassuring the artist that he doesn't live entirely in the past.

But in the way they organize their set lists the performers

themselves make it clear that they know what the twelve tracks are. Bruce Springsteen will be remembered for 'Born To Run' as surely as Wordsworth is remembered for 'Daffodils'. Radiohead will be remembered for 'No Surprises' as surely as Coleridge is for *The Rime of the Ancient Mariner*. And they both know it.

They know that their career is one thing but their best songs have a life that is greater than that career. The songs you're remembered for are the songs that are more famous than you are. Often the writer isn't remembered at all. That's the deal you enter into when you write a real classic. It goes out into the world without you.

For all his well-advertised unpredictability, Bob Dylan still goes out and performs his twelve songs. 'A song is anything that can walk by itself,' he wrote in 1965.

A songwriter who's come up with twelve that can do that should be proud.

FIFTEEN
MEMORABLE GIGS

1. **Chuck Berry in Bradford**

   Google plays havoc with the tidy garden of memory but it's here now so I have to use it. This was my first proper gig. I thought it was 1965. Google tells me it was actually 1964. I thought it was the Bradford Alhambra. It was actually the Bradford Gaumont. The Animals played a song they said they were about to record. It was called 'House Of The Rising Sun'. Chuck did his standard half-hour backed by Kingsize Taylor and the Dominoes. If I'm honest it didn't sound very good. Nevertheless just to see him and that big red guitar was enthralling enough.

2. **Little Feat in London**

   This was in January 1975. The Warner Brothers Music Show was a package tour headlined by the Doobie Brothers. The only act anyone really wanted to see were Little Feat, who were the cognoscenti's favourite at the time. Their only show in London was supporting the Doobies on a Sunday afternoon. They came on in the early afternoon in front of a packed house and received such an ecstatic reaction that they were actually embarrassed. At the end they did as many encores as a support group decently could. When the Doobie Brothers came on people left in the most calculated display of snubbing I've ever seen. I learned something important about rock fans that day: they really love something to be against.

3. Yes in London

This show took place at the LSE in February 1971. Student gigs were cheap but always uncomfortable, particularly because the longer the audience's hair the more likely they were to sit down. Yes were the first group to have their own PA. In those days, when the sound was acceptable people always came away saying, 'They had their own PA, you know.'

4. Elvis Costello in London

In the summer of 1977 Elvis Costello and the Attractions played a weekly residency at the Nashville in West Kensington on Sunday nights. This was a uniquely exciting time because each week they would play new songs they had written during the week. Elvis was enjoying being able to get away with everything. During this period I took him to do a session at Capital Radio and he played 'Radio Radio'. One line goes 'the radio's in the hands of such a lot of fools who want to anaesthetize the way you feel'. The session was being supervised by the station's head of music.

5. **Toumani Diabaté in Mali**

I was out in Mali in 2008 doing a story for *The Word* on the great kora master. I actually did the interview sitting in his front yard as night fell. When it got dark – Africa dark, that is – he took out his instrument and just played for me. It was magically quiet. I was a one-man audience. The only illumination came from a series of cigarettes, each of which he sparked with his gold lighter.

6. **Louis Armstrong in Batley**

In 1967 the old variety theatres had gone and the most lucrative gigs were on the northern circuit of what had once been called 'working men's clubs'. The most gold-plated of these was the Batley Variety Club, which is where I ended up seeing Louis Armstrong and what remained of his all-stars playing a few of his old classics plus 'Hello Dolly', which was a big hit at the time. The longer time goes on the more amazing it seems to me that I saw him.

7. **Van Morrison and the Caledonia Soul Orchestra in London**

Thanks to the live album *It's Too Late To Stop Now* the worldwide community of Van Morrison fans have been able to enjoy this concert which took place at the Rainbow in the summer of 1973. The young men who were actually there still haven't got over the sight and sound of Van's cellist Terry Adams. She was sited downstage, largely invisible beneath a waist-length curtain of the most perfect long blonde hair. She had bare, beautiful arms. Terry distracted us from the fact that we were witnessing the brief window when Van Morrison actually enjoyed live performing. We didn't know it wouldn't last.

8. **Paul McCartney at Earls Court**

I'm not one of those people who make a habit of taking their offspring to gigs on the grounds that it will be good for them. They'll find music like I did, on their own. However, in 2003 I'd just done a job for Paul McCartney's organization and he was due to play in London. I was told I could take the family. I asked the 'kids', who at the time were twenty, fifteen and ten, if they fancied it. They didn't just fancy it. They were very keen. And thus when he came on and started with 'Hello Goodbye', 'All My Loving' and 'Getting Better' there we all were, effectively watching the Beatles. They say the best times as a family are when you're together but can't actually talk to each other. That was one of the best times.

9. **Live Aid**

I wasn't in the crowd at Wembley Stadium on 13 July 1985. I spent most of my time in the commentary position which in those days was high up in the eaves of the old stand. I still feel that the reason this lives so long in the memory was nothing to do with Queen or any of the other acts. It was because it took place on that most exceptional of days, a sunny afternoon in England. It was the resulting TV pictures that persuaded the average Briton that they really should start going to big open-air megashows.

10. **Ian Dury and the Blockheads in Sheffield**

The year was 1980 and *Do It Yourself*, their follow-up to *New Boots And Panties!!*, had recently been released. Following a brilliant show at the City Hall we all got on a bus to go to the hotel in Leeds. As we waited in the venue car park for a few stragglers I saw something I have not seen before or since. One member of the band simply beckoned to a female fan from inside the bus. Immediately, without further bidding, she climbed aboard, joined him and came back to the hotel. On the way to Leeds the Linda Lovelace film *Deep Throat* was screened on the bus's TV. Different times.

11. Geno Washington and the Ram Jam Band in Leeds

In the year 1967 it was considered perfectly normal to like, say, Country Joe and the Fish without that in any way lessening your love of soul music in the Southern tradition. The person who purveyed this live in the UK was Geno Washington, a former US serviceman who did an acceptable Eddie Floyd around the ballrooms of the North, frequently playing more than one city in a night. Not long after I saw him do his stuff in this overcrowded Mecca ballroom I happened to be on my way to a party in a suburb of Leeds when a minibus pulled up alongside me and a black man in the passenger seat asked, 'Which way is Bradford?' I pointed and off they went. That's how I can say I met Geno Washington.

12. Crowded House in Sydney, Australia

On 23 November 1996 Crowded House were due to play their last show at a free concert on Bennelong Point, the promontory that is home to the Sydney Opera House. On the appointed day it rained heavily, as it frequently does in Sydney, so the big show was postponed until the following day for safety reasons. However many hundreds of people had travelled long distances to be there and were due to fly back in the morning so the band played their entire show for those people. On the following day, which was fine, hundreds of thousands of people flooded on to Bennelong Point and they played the show proper, climaxing with a firework display over the harbour bridge. Because nothing in rock and roll truly finishes any more they inevitably did it again twenty years later.

13. The Dixie Chicks in London

I went to this show at the Shepherd's Bush Empire in March 2003 out of curiosity. During some between-songs patter Natalie Maines made the mildest possible remark about apologizing for George Bush coming from Texas. In the house on the night it passed barely noticed. When it landed back in the United States it all but finished their career. This was the first intimation of the new age where what happens doesn't matter as much as what people think happened. In this madly censorious time both left and right like nothing more than to whip up fake indignation to draw people to their pulpits.

14. Elton John at Wembley Stadium

Elton tends to blame his more hubristic moments on the devil's dandruff. That must have been one of the factors persuading him it would be a good idea to go out in front of eighty thousand people who had been baking in the sun on this midsummer Saturday in 1974 and play the whole of his new album *Captain Fantastic And The Brown Dirt Cowboy* in the same order as it was on the record. It was made worse by the fact that it hadn't been out long enough for the audience to be familiar with it. It was made doubly bad because he came on after the Beach Boys performing what was at the time the most appealing greatest hits set in the world. This was an early intimation that there is no entertainer more capable of ignoring what the mood of the audience should be telling him than the newly minted rock superstar.

15. Bob Dylan in Hollywood

It was the summer of 1992. I was in Los Angeles to interview Bruce Springsteen who was rehearsing his new band. We had arrived in the midst of Bob Dylan's week at the Pantages Theatre, a splendid deco movie place on Hollywood Boulevard. Everybody assured us that Dylan was miraculously at the top of his game. Therefore for the only time in my life I paid a scalper and got in. I was sitting next to Mark Cooper of BBC Television. The show began. It was no different from other Dylan shows I'd seen around that time. Impossible to tell one number from another. At one point he started a new one and Mark and I turned to each other and said brightly, ' "All Along The Watchtower".' After a few bars we turned back to each other and said, 'No, it's "Don't Think Twice, It's All Right".' Two days later at breakfast I bumped into Springsteen's manager Jon Landau who told me he and Bruce had been to Dylan the night before. 'You know, it was really funny. At one point Bruce and I turned to each other and said, " 'All Along The Watchtower' . . ." '

SEVEN THINGS I WOULD TELL A YOUNG BAND

I've never been in a rock band but I've stood and watched enough up-and-coming bands perform to have realized a few things the people in those bands still don't appear to have realized. The other night I saw another lot of up-and-comers and found myself thinking the same things I've thought for years.

1. The most precious resource is not your music, it's the audience's attention, and therefore you shouldn't allow the latter to drop for so much as a second.

2. Please introduce yourself or be introduced. Nobody gets points for being modest. Bob Dylan has a man whose job it is to list his achievements and remind the audience who he is before he comes on. And he's Bob Bloody Dylan.

3. Get on stage and start at least two minutes before your agreed time. And for God's sake, don't faff. In their early days Elvis Costello and the Attractions would run on clutching the tools of their trade, which was a signal. Any band who didn't want to waste their own time were unlikely to waste yours either.

4. Audiences only really like two parts of a show – the beginning and the end. You should prolong the former by rolling directly through your first three numbers without pausing. Then make sure you end suddenly and unexpectedly. Audiences reward bands who stop early and punish those who stay late.

5. Between songs, never approach the microphone and say the first thing that comes into your head. The chat is as important as the music. The audience wants to feel that somebody is in charge. If it isn't you they will take charge, and you won't like that one little bit.

6. In his excellent book *The Ten Rules of Rock and Roll*, Robert Forster says, 'No band does anything new on stage after the first twenty minutes.' Try to prove him wrong by doing one thing the audience is not expecting you to do. That's what the people will talk about on the way home.

7. Finally, there's nothing an audience enjoys more than hearing something familiar. If you think your songwriting and all-round musical excellence are enough to entertain a bunch of strangers for an hour with songs they have never heard before, bully for you. The Beatles didn't, but what the hell did they know?

TWENTY SONGS ABOUT AMERICANS ON THE MOVE

You can't travel more than a few hundred miles in the UK without falling off the edge of the country. That could be why relatively few British songs are about the business of moving while so many American ones are. Moving to a new career in a new town is so much a part of the American experience that we Europeans actively look forward to the inevitable scene in the movie where the heroine packs everything into a U-Haul trailer and travels thousands of miles to she knows not what. This is something foreign to our experience but we nonetheless identify with the admixture of excitement and sadness attending such a move. This is especially true when this feeling is expressed in a song.

Whole areas of American popular song are about moving from country to city, from city to city, and from city back to the theoretical peace of the rural life. Music has soundtracked all the migrations large and small that make the American story. Music has also made American place names more famous overseas than they are at home. We're accustomed to every last backing musician in American touring bands being introduced on stage with a reference to their place of birth. The smaller that place is the more important it seems that it should get a mention.

We have internalized the names of places along with the songs that were associated with them. Anybody with a smattering of familiarity with American popular music knows Tulsa, Pasadena, Chattanooga, Muscle Shoals, San Jose, Asbury Park, Clarksdale, Baltimore, Wichita, Galveston, Route 66, Highway 61, the New Jersey Turnpike and even the corner of Lexington and 125th Street. A passionate minority know Kokomo, Barrytown, Johnstown, Ventura, Union City, Flagstaff, even Tehachapi and Tonopah. A few enthusiasts may even have traced the route taken by Chuck Berry in 'Promised Land' on a map.

I'm one of the latter group. Without meaning to I've acquired a basic education in the map of America over the years purely from listening to American pop music. In addition I've learned that each of those journeys described in each of these songs has some special significance. It's rarely the fastest route between two musical-sounding places on the map. Each journey is being taken for a reason, and knowing that reason, or at least guessing at it, helps turn each song into a small movie. What follows is a list of twenty personal favourites.

1. **Gladys Knight & The Pips: 'Midnight Train To Georgia'**
   This is actually a song about LA. That's the place he's leaving because, as the song's unique opening line has it, it 'proved

too much for the man'. The original wisp of an idea for the song came from a phone conversation between the writer, Jim Weatherly, and the actress Farrah Fawcett Majors, during which she told him she was catching the midnight plane to Houston. Like all great records it's unimaginable now in any other shape than the one it ended up in.

2. **Tom T. Hall: 'That's How I Got To Memphis'**
One of the reasons the British don't write much about their own cities is that few of the place names are as euphonious as Memphis. There are myriad versions of this song, many of them good, but this by the writer is the original. Guy marries woman from Memphis, they live out in the middle of nowhere, she gets mad and walks out and so he follows her to Memphis 'to find out the trouble she's in'. You can tell from the tone of his voice that he probably won't find her.

3. **Jonathan Richman: 'You're Crazy For Taking The Bus'**
Jonathan was a believer in the new asceticism long before most musicians: vegetables over meat, acoustic over electric, pedal power over the petrol engine. On the face of it this is a characteristic commercial for taking the bus rather than the plane, thereby saving yourself money and aggravation at the airport. It's also an argument for doing something that travelling musicians tend to avoid doing, which is engaging with the welfare gals, drunk galoots and muttering misfits who make up the real America you can find on a Greyhound bus.

4. **Randy Newman: 'Sail Away'**
Randy Newman often puts his best words in the mouths of his most reprehensible protagonists, and there's none more

reprehensible than this West African slaver supposedly advertising the benefits of transportation in chains. Newman also puts some of his most affecting music to work singing the praises of how it will feel to finally enter Charleston Bay. The chances of anyone entertaining this kind of thought in popular music today seem slim, the chances of them couching it in such warm, seductive terms non-existent.

5. **Bob Seger: 'Roll Me Away'**
On the face of it this song is nothing more than a preposterous middle-aged man's fantasy, such as might have sprung from the febrile imaginings of Madison Avenue and been used to sell beer. You leave behind your responsibilities, take off on your motorbike with a strange woman and keep searching till you find what's right. Only Bob Seger has the quality of heart to redeem it, and in Roy Bittan he has the pianist to ensure no heart string remains unplucked.

6. **Simon & Garfunkel: 'America'**
There's a strain of delicious self-pity that accompanies long-distance travel. It's a state that encourages fantasies in which the traveller has some noble purpose. Paul Simon's 'America' is a perfect expression of this altered state. Here he is with his girlfriend, Cathy from Brentford in Essex. The two of them have caught the Greyhound in Pittsburgh and now that they're in sight of New York he's feeling 'empty and aching and I don't know why'. This was the key track of *Bookends* and its enduring popularity explains why, even fifty years later, at least one car on the New Jersey Turnpike will have a passenger staring out of the window with a melancholy air, silently counting the cars as they pass.

7. **Jan & Dean: 'Surf City'**
Brian Wilson, who co-wrote this, never surfed. We kids in the north of England who thrilled to it in 1963 barely knew what surfing was. It didn't matter. We just responded to its message of escape into a world of perpetual sunshine where, as they promised in the first line, there were 'two girls for every boy'. Surf City didn't exist, of course, but its promise is eternal.

8. **Eddie Floyd: 'Big Bird'**
The story goes that Eddie Floyd wrote this on the tarmac at Heathrow while waiting for the plane to take him home to Otis Redding's funeral in 1967. Once you've heard it you won't be able to take a flight again without urging your plane through its agonizing ascent into the skies with the words 'get on up, Big Bird'.

9. **Jackson Browne: 'The Late Show'**
The song's about persuading a woman to go away with him. The last verse, which was actually visualized on the cover of the album *Late For The Sky*, has him parked across the street from her home in an early-model Chevrolet. Will she go with him? As the final instrumental playout swells we hear a car door slamming. Then a pause. Then another door. Bruce Springsteen says it makes him cry every time.

10. **Bruce Springsteen: 'Thunder Road'**
Lots of the best pop songs are about people making an entrance. In the real world lots of them are used to steel the listener to make an entrance. Springsteen's used this trope more than once but never more cinematically than in this song which begins with the girl dancing across the porch to

meet her lover. He even specifies the music that's playing. It's Roy Orbison. The lover is parked outside and promises to either show her a good time or, this being Bruce Springsteen, conduct her from the world of darkness to the world of light.

11. Chuck Berry: 'Promised Land'

Precious few pop songs have endings as thrillingly neat as this account of a rounder's trip from Norfolk, Virginia to Los Angeles, California. Upon arrival after many adventures he asks the operator to reverse the charges to Tidewater 4-10-09 and 'tell the folks back home this is the Promised Land calling and the poor boy's on the line'. In my imagination, as he waits to be put through he buffs his nails to a sheen on the lapel of his powder blue suit.

12. Emmylou Harris: 'Boulder To Birmingham'

I've loved this song ever since I first heard it in 1975. It's about Harris missing her partner Gram Parsons, who died in 1973. In it she promises that she would walk all the way from Boulder to Birmingham if only she could see his face. It was only recently while listening to a Malcolm Gladwell podcast that I understood that the two cities aren't just chosen because they begin with a B. They also represent the distance between two Americas, the liberal university town in the Rockies and the home of the segregated South. It's in songs like this one that geography, politics and history collide.

13. Little Feat: 'Willin''

Lowell George was the son of a wealthy Hollywood furrier. He knew as much about trucking as Brad Pitt knows about fist fighting. Despite this, his impression of a grimly determined knight of the road hauling heavy goods through the Californian desert on a diet of weed, whites and wine is more moving than a mere pastiche. Once he'd written it he had to play it every night.

14. Steve Miller Band: 'Mercury Blues'

In the first thirty years of rock and roll it was axiomatic that the guy who had the coolest car always got the girl. These days nobody talks about car envy any more. This suggests there's a conspiracy of silence around the subject or we have reached a higher evolutionary plane. Miller, who's done his share of songs about cool methods of transport, delivers an icy hymn to the vehicle in which he plans to cruise up and down this road.

15. Rosanne Cash: 'Runaway Train'

This is magnificent. John Stewart wrote the song, which is about a relationship that has gone badly wrong. Cash sings it with utter conviction. Stewart extends the locomotive metaphor brilliantly throughout the song. 'To try to get off now is about as insane as those who wave lanterns at runaway trains.' Of course none of us have ever seen a runaway train but it's an idea too powerful to pass up.

16. Dionne Warwick: 'Do You Know The Way To San Jose'

The songs about not making it in Hollywood are invariably more interesting than the ones about success. Dionne Warwick had to be persuaded to record this. She still thinks it's a dumb song. She's wrong. As long as Hollywood continues to attract a new generation of wannabes who end up parking cars and pumping gas it never will be.

17. Harry McClintock: 'Big Rock Candy Mountain'

When I was a child, radio would play a bowdlerized version of this song about the hobo life. In that version the cigarette trees became peppermint trees and the streams ran with lemonade rather than alcohol. McClintock claimed to have originated the song in the late 1920s but its roots go back into the nineteenth century. It's a celebration of the life of the resourceful itinerant dodging the dogs of the railroad police, which was a strain of American culture long before Bob Dylan was ever heard of.

18. J. Blackfoot: 'Taxi'

It begins with the sound of rain falling on a city street. Blackfoot needs to get to his baby and deliver an apology for his misbehaviour. A phone call won't do. A text is not an option. He's having difficulty finding a cab that will take him to the other side of town. Then he spies one across the street and, being a streetwise individual, he hails it with a piercing whistle. Cue the song.

19. Lucinda Williams: 'Car Wheels On A Gravel Road'

Our first experience of travel is as unwilling passengers in the backs of cars driven by our parents. The purpose of the journey is often unknown to us but appears urgent to the people in the front seat. Lucinda Williams' haunting song recounts just one of these journeys. We're no wiser at the end than we were at the beginning but the sound of those tyres will stay with us for ever.

20. The Godchildren of Soul featuring General Johnson and Joey Ramone: 'Rockaway Beach'

Rockaway Beach is at the southern end of Long Island in an area that used to be known as the Irish Riviera. When the Ramones sang about its glories we never believed that they had been there, let alone surfed; and when General Johnson, formerly of the Chairmen of the Board, did his own 'beach music' version of it in 1994 we never thought he'd been near the water either. Nevertheless the idea of taking that trip was the exciting thing. Ultimately it's the idea that mattered.

FIVE RECORDS THAT ALWAYS WORK AT WEDDINGS

Here's a test for you.

The DJ hired to entertain the crowd at your family wedding is held up in traffic and won't be able to attend. He has, however, taken the precaution of ordering every record ever made and sending them on ahead. And you – yes, you – have been chosen from literally millions of people to provide the soundtrack to this evening. This will either ensure everyone attending has a memorable couple of hours or you'll be responsible for getting the couple's marriage off to the kind of start from which it would be surprising to see any relationship recover.

Your job is to make sure that everyone, from the small children currently sliding up and down the highly polished floor of the hotel ballroom to the bride's co-workers who have been augmenting their champagne intake with shots of tequila and are now casting a critical eye over the erection of the PA system, is for a short while, in the words of Sister Sledge, lost in music. In the next few minutes your selection from the millions of possibilities involved must make this otherwise disparate sampling of humanity magically coalesce and, in the words of Brinsley Schwarz, surrender to the rhythm.

Now is not the time to bandy genres. Now is not the time to succumb to the crippling maw of cool. Forget about hard house or handbag. These people standing before you are simple human souls: excitable teenagers who've been drinking too much, little girls who want to twirl and twirl until they go red and throw up, tipsy aunts in their sixties aching to prove their day is not entirely past, middle-aged dads craving permission to unleash the sexy beast that once got them a knee trembler on the way home from a college ball, and also, I can guarantee, some smirking young blokes at the bar wanting it all to go Pete Tong.

Here's my first piece of advice, culled from long experience of observing the human animal at play in the dancing situation. Don't for a moment do anything to appease those smirking young blokes. Put them out of your mind. You could select the coolest tune in the world, the very one they've just downloaded, and they still won't dance because these people are in the grip of a level of inhibition unseen since the days of Cromwell.

In fact I'll go further. Don't do anything at all to appease the younger slice of the demographic (unless it's the ten-year-olds who do at least drag Dad on the floor with them) because none of it will work.

No, the swing voters in this dance constituency are your

middle-aged. If you can get them across the threshold of their self-consciousness – about their shape, their age, their hairline, their trousers, their mortgage, the fact that their kids are watching – and on to that dance floor, they will chairlift you home in gratitude at the end of the evening. Get them up and frugging and it will only be nanoseconds before the lovely young women throw off their agonizing shoes in a shared squeal of relief and delight and leap in after them, secure in the knowledge that next to their dads and uncles there's no way they can end up looking stupid. And where the lovely young women lead the smirking young men follow, generally four Stellas later.

So, hey, Mr DJ, you approach the stand, your heart in your mouth, and consider your first five tunes. Here you're on your own. You make your own selection. These are mine, honed in the hard school and burnished in debate only the other day, in conversation with a wide demographic span at a friend's barbecue.

1. **'Dancing Queen' by Abba**

    There isn't a person in your room who doesn't love this record – plus it's just cheesy enough for the men to convince themselves they're somehow dancing satirically.

2. **'Open Your Heart' by Madonna**

    In these circumstances you should avoid anything less than ten years old. The temptation to play the new one must be resisted at every juncture. Nobody will thank you for it. The great thing about 'Open Your Heart' is it begins with the clatter of familiarity that propels people out of their seat more effectively than a whoopee cushion.

3. **'Dancing In The Dark' by Bruce Springsteen**

   You need a song which is about dancing because it subliminally helps people justify the strange convulsions their body is performing.

4. **'The Jean Genie' by David Bowie**

   It's rock but not Rock. Important difference. Rock in a disco is Death.

5. **'Jump Around' by House of Pain**

   This has that rare quality of being utterly familiar even to people who've never heard it before, and the blokes, for whom dancing is a branch of the martial arts, can put their fists in the air and join in the 'jump, jump, jump, jump' bit.

What else? The following should probably be given a wide berth: the Beatles (in fact, much as it pains me, anything that pre-dates the early seventies), anything from the last ten years, anything with a long instrumental section, anything you don't recognize immediately, most white British bands except the Stones, anything designed to appease the rock snobs, any intriguing new mix that shows the song in an entirely new light, anything that sounded great in the dance tent at Glastonbury when you were off your head, anything you would really like more people to hear and, most crucially of all, anything longer than three minutes fifty seconds' duration. Apart from that, nothing is ruled out. No, not even 'The Birdie Song'. If it works, it works.

INDEX

Index

Index

Index

Index

Index

A FABULOUS CREATION
How LPs Saved Our Lives

David Hepworth

The era of the LP began in 1967, with *Sgt. Pepper*; the Beatles didn't just collect together a bunch of songs, they Made An Album. Henceforth, everybody else wanted to Make An Album.

The end came only fifteen years later, coinciding with the release of Michael Jackson's *Thriller*. By then the Walkman had taken music out of the home and into the streets, and the record business had begun trying to reverse-engineer the creative process in order to make big money. Nobody would play music or listen to it in quite the same way ever again.

It was a short but transformative time. Musicians became 'artists' and we, the people, patrons of the arts. The LP itself had been a mark of sophistication, a measure of wealth, an instrument of education, a poster saying things you dare not say yourself, a means of attracting the opposite sex, and, for many, the single most desirable object in their lives.

This is the story of that time; it takes us from recording studios where musicians were doing things that had never been done before to the sparsely furnished apartments where their efforts would be received like visitations from a higher power. This is the story of how LPs saved our lives.

OUT MARCH 2019